Commentary on Ezra, Nehemiah, and Esther
Bible Study Notes and Comments

by David E. Pratte

Available in print at
www.lighttomypath.net/sales

Commentary on Ezra, Nehemiah, and Esther:
Bible Study Notes and Comments

© Copyright David E. Pratte, 2009, 2013
(minor revisions, 2016)
All rights reserved

ISBN-13: 978-1494819965
ISBN-10: 1494819961

Printed books, booklets, and tracts available at
www.lighttomypath.net/sales
Free Bible study articles online at
www.gospelway.com
Free Bible courses online at
www.biblestudylessons.com
Free class books at
www.biblestudylessons.com/classbooks
Free commentaries on Bible books at
www.gospelway.com/commentary
Contact the author at
www.gospelway.com/comments

Note carefully: No teaching in any of our materials is intended or should ever be construed to justify or to in any way incite or encourage personal vengeance or physical violence against any person.

Front page photo

Statue of two-headed bull from ancient Persia in the time of King Xerxes (housed in the Oriental Institute). Xerxes is the Greek name for Ahasuerus who married Esther.

Other Books by the Author

Topical Bible Studies

Growing a Godly Marriage & Raising Godly Children
Why Believe in God, Jesus, and the Bible? (evidences)
The God of the Bible (study of the Father, Son, and Holy Spirit)
Grace, Faith, and Obedience: The Gospel or Calvinism?
Kingdom of Christ: Future Millennium or Present Spiritual Reign?
Do Not Sin Against the Child: Abortion, Unborn Life, & the Bible
True Words of God: Bible Inspiration and Preservation

Commentaries

Commentary on the Book of Genesis
Commentary on the Books of Joshua and Ruth
Commentary on the Book of Judges
Commentary on Ezra, Nehemiah, and Esther
Commentary on Job
Commentary on Proverbs
Commentary on the Gospel of Mark
Commentary on the Gospel of John
Commentary on the Book of Acts
Commentary on the Book of Hebrews

Bible Question Class Books

Genesis	*Gospel of John*
Joshua and Ruth	*Acts*
Judges	*Romans*
1 Samuel	*1 Corinthians*
Ezra, Nehemiah, and Esther	*2 Corinthians and Galatians*
Job	*Ephesians and Philippians*
Proverbs	*Colossians, 1&2 Thessalonians*
Isaiah	*1 & 2 Timothy, Titus, Philemon*
Gospel of Matthew	*Hebrews*
Gospel of Mark	*General Epistles (James - Jude)*
Gospel of Luke	*Revelation*

Workbooks with Study Notes

Jesus Is Lord: Workbook on the Fundamentals of the Gospel of Christ
Following Jesus: Workbook on Discipleship
God's Eternal Purpose in Christ: Workbook on the Theme of the Bible

Table of Contents

Introduction to the Book of Ezra..6
Ezra Chapter 1..11
Ezra Chapter 2..14
Ezra Chapter 3..16
Ezra Chapter 4..20
Ezra Chapter 5..26
Ezra Chapter 6..31
Ezra Chapter 7..35
Ezra Chapter 8..39
Ezra Chapter 9..43
Ezra Chapter 10..47
Introduction to the Book of Nehemiah 53
Nehemiah Chapter 1 57
Nehemiah Chapter 2..62
Nehemiah Chapter 3..69
Nehemiah Chapter 4..70
Nehemiah Chapter 5..79
Nehemiah Chapter 6..87
Nehemiah Chapter 7..97
Nehemiah Chapter 8 99
Nehemiah Chapter 9...104
Nehemiah Chapter 10...112
Nehemiah Chapter 11...117
Nehemiah Chapter 12 120
Nehemiah Chapter 13 124
Introduction to the Book of Esther...134
Esther Chapter 1..136
Esther Chapter 2..140
Esther Chapter 3..145
Esther Chapter 4..151
Esther Chapter 5..159
Esther Chapter 6..164
Esther Chapter 7..169
Esther Chapter 8 175
Esther Chapter 9..180
Esther Chapter 10 186
(Due to printer reformatting, the above numbers may be off a page or two.)

Notes to the Reader

To save space and for other reasons, I have chosen not to include the Bible text in these notes (please use your Bible to follow along). When I do quote a Scripture, I generally quote the New King James Version, unless otherwise indicated. Often – especially when I do not use quotations marks – I am not quoting any translation but simply paraphrasing the passage in my own words. Also, when I ask the reader to refer to a map, please consult the maps at the back of your Bible or in a Bible dictionary.

You can find study questions to accompany these notes at www.lighttomypath.net/sales

To join our mailing list to be informed of new books or special sales, contact the author at www.gospelway.com/comments

Introductory Thoughts about Commentaries

Only the Scriptures provide an infallible, authoritatively inspired revelation of God's will for man (2 Timothy 3:16,17). It follows that this commentary, like all commentaries, was written by an uninspired, fallible human. It is the author's effort to share his insights about God's word for the purpose of instructing and edifying others in the knowledge and wisdom found in Scripture. It is simply another form of teaching, like public preaching, Bible class teaching, etc., except in written form (like tracts, Bible class literature, etc.). Nehemiah 8:8; Ephesians 4:15,16; Romans 15:14; 1 Thessalonians 5:11; Hebrews 3:12-14; 5:12-14; 10:23-25; Romans 10:17; Mark 16:15,16; Acts 8:4; 2 Timothy 2:2,24-26; 4:2-4; 1 Peter 3:15.

It follows that the student must read any commentary with discernment, realizing that any fallible teacher may err, whether he is teaching orally or in writing. So, the student must compare all spiritual teaching to the truth of God's word (Acts 17:11). It may be wise to read several commentaries to consider alternative views on difficult points. But it is especially important to consider the *reasons or evidence* each author gives for his views, then compare them to the Bible.

For these reasons, the author urges the reader to always consider my comments in light of Scripture. Accept what I say only if you find that it harmonizes with God's word. And please do not cite my writings as authority, as though people should accept anything I say as authoritative. Always let the Bible be your authority.

"He who glories, let him glory in the Lord" – 1 Corinthians 1:31

Abbreviations Used in These Notes

ASV – American Standard Version
b/c/v – book, chapter, and verse
ESV – English Standard Version
f – the following verse
ff – the following verses
KJV – King James Version
NASB – New American Standard Bible
NEB – New English Bible
NIV – New International Version
NKJV – New King James Version
RSV – Revised Standard Version

Introduction to the Book of Ezra

Background of the Book

Theme
Ezra and Nehemiah give the historical accounts of the return of the Jews from Babylonian captivity. Ezra records the events relating to the first two groups, and discusses especially the rebuilding of the temple.

Author
The inspired author is generally believed to be Ezra. Horne says:

> It is evident that the author of the book of Ezra was personally present at the transactions recorded in it, the narrative being in the first person ... That the last four chapters of this book were written by Ezra himself there can be' no doubt, as he particularly describes himself in the beginning of the seventh chapter, and likewise frequently introduces himself in the subsequent chapters. The Jews, indeed, ascribe the whole of this book to Ezra, and their opinion is adopted by most Christian commentators.

Summary of book by sections:
Chapter 1-6 — Rebuilding of the temple
Chapter 7-10 — Return of Ezra and purifying the people from foreign wives

Summary of events by chapter:
Chapter 1 — The decree of Cyrus that the Jews could return (536 BC)
Chapter 2 — Names of those who return
Chapter 3 — Laying of the foundation of the temple
Chapter 4 — The people of the land oppose the work and move the king to stop it

Chapter 5 — Prophets encourage the work to resume; inquiry is made of King Darius

Chapter 6 — Darius decreed to allow the work; the temple completed

Chapter 7 — Ezra decreed to lead another group to return (458 BC)

Chapter 8 — Preparation and journey

Chapter 9,10 — The people put away wives and children of foreign blood (compare Deut. 7:2,3; Exodus. 34:15,16; Josh. 23:12f; Neh. 13:23-27)

Contemporary prophets

Haggai and Zechariah lived during this period and helped motivate the people in the work. (See Ezra 5:1,2; 6:14,15.)

Historical Setting

Events in Ezra and Nehemiah occurred during the period of the Jews' return from Babylonian captivity. When the Babylonians had captured Jerusalem and overthrown the nation of Judah, they took the Jews into captivity away from Palestine into Babylon (see 2 Chronicles 36:11-21). But the Medes and Persians later overthrew the Babylonians and began a policy of allowing the Jews to return to Palestine.

There were actually three groups that returned. The first group returned in 536 BC under leadership of Zerubbabel, the second group in 458 BC led by Ezra, and the third group in 445 BC led by Nehemiah.

Consider the history of the period according to the reigns of several great Persian kings (note 4:3-7):

Cyrus — He overthrew Babylon in 538 BC. The first group of Jews returned to Palestine under Zerubbabel's leadership in 536 BC.

Darius the "Great" — During his lifetime, the temple in Jerusalem was rebuilt.

Xerxes — This is the Ahasuerus of the book of Esther. He eventually chose Esther as his queen, and by her influence the Jews were saved from destruction.

Artaxerxes — This man was son of Xerxes and stepson of Esther. He ruled from about 465-423 BC. The books of Ezra and Nehemiah were written during his reign.

Ezra's record begins with the first group that returned under Cyrus. But Ezra himself became personally involved in the story during the 7th year of the reign of Artaxerxes, when Ezra led a group of Jews back to Palestine (458 BC). In the 21st year of the reign, Nehemiah led another group of Jews to return, and rebuilt the walls of Jerusalem.

Practical Lessons

In many ways, the time of Ezra and Nehemiah was like our own. God's people had been in apostasy, which led to the Babylonian captivity. Some leaders had begun the work of restoring the people to God's service, but there were still many problems and the people continued to fall into sin. The task of Ezra and Nehemiah was to provide leadership to continue the restoration and to challenge the people to spiritual faithfulness.

Similarly under the New Testament, after the first century God's church went into apostasy resulting in the Catholic and Protestant churches. In our age, God's people have sought to return to God and to restore the church. But there are still many problems and God's people often continue to fall into sin. Strong and faithful leaders are needed to continue the restoration and to challenge God's people to spiritual faithfulness.

We can learn many practical lessons from the problems Ezra and Nehemiah faced and how they dealt with them by God's help.

Part 1: Rebuilding of the Temple – Chapter 1-6

Ezra Chapter 1

The Decree of Cyrus that the Jews Could Return (536 BC) – Chapter 1

1:1,2 – *Cyrus, king of Persia, decreed that the Jews could return and rebuild the temple.*

After Babylon fell to the Persians, the first king of the Persian Empire was Cyrus. Various Old Testament prophets, including Jeremiah, had predicted the defeat of the Babylonians by the Persians (Jeremiah 25:12-14; 29:10-14; compare Daniel 5).

God then motivated Cyrus to send the Jews back to Jerusalem so they could rebuild the temple. This is also recorded in 2 Chronicles 36:20-23. We are not told exactly how God so moved Cyrus. God works by His providence in ways we do not understand. But Isaiah had prophesied this would happen, even calling Cyrus by name (Isaiah 44:24-45:7).

Waldron points out that this was a general decree stating a general policy of Cyrus and the Persians. The Babylonians had taken captured people away from their homelands and resettled them elsewhere. But the Persians sought to gain favor and peace among their captives by allowing them to return to their homelands, rebuild their temples, and re-establish worship of their gods.

Joseph Free states that this policy of Cyrus is confirmed by archaeology. Many written records have been discovered from the time of Cyrus, including the Cyrus Cylinder. In this record, Cyrus stated: "All of their peoples I assembled and restored to their own dwelling places."

Holden and Geisler confirm this evidence regarding Cyrus and also point out that the tomb of Cyrus still exists and is well known in Iran (page 279).

1:3-6 – *Those who returned were to bring provisions.*

In the case of the Jews, Cyrus decreed that God had commanded him to build the house for God at Jerusalem. So he authorized two things to accomplish this:

(1) Some of the Jews were to go back to Jerusalem from captivity to build the temple.

(2) Those who remained in their places of sojourning (i.e., captives who did not return) were to help finance the effort by giving gold, silver, goods, and livestock by freewill offerings.

Waldron also points out that Persia ruled the entire area (and more) that had been controlled earlier by the Assyrians and then by the Babylonians. So the decree in principle would have allowed, not just the people from the southern nation of Judah to return, but also people from the northern nation of Israel or Samaria. However, only those who were willing to go did so. We will see that this included generally those from the southern nation of Judah.

The people did as Cyrus decreed. Some determined to go to Jerusalem to build the temple. Others determined to help financially by providing silver, gold, goods, and livestock.

Note that those who actually did return were basically of the tribes of Judah and Benjamin, along with some priests and other Levites (of the tribe of Levi). These were stirred in spirit by God to return. As with Cyrus, this would not necessarily mean direct revelation. They could have been stirred by longing for their homeland, by remembrance of the promises God had made to the nation, by the prophecies of Jeremiah and others, or even by other prophets who urged them to go.

1:7-11 – *The people were permitted to bring back the furnishings from the destroyed temple.*

Cyrus himself gave back all the articles of value taken by Nebuchadnezzar from the temple. These are described in some detail, demonstrating the great value of what had been in the temple, and the considerable sacrifice Cyrus made in giving it back. A total of 5400 articles of gold and silver were returned.

These articles had been taken when the Babylonians captured Jerusalem and placed in the heathen temples of Babylon (2 Chronicles 36:7,18; Daniel 1:2; Ezra 5:14; 6:5). Later, as recorded in Daniel 5, Belshazzar had used them in an idolatrous feast. At that time God sent a moving hand to write on the wall a warning to Belshazzar that his doom was sealed. Daniel interpreted the meaning of the message, and that night the Persians overthrew Babylon.

These same articles were apparently now to be restored to their place in a rebuilt temple in Jerusalem at the decree of Cyrus. So they were put in the care of one named Sheshbazzar to return. He did so, as shown in 5:14,16. Sheshbazzar is here called a prince of Judah. 5:14 says he was made governor of the land, and 5:16 says he began the rebuilding of the temple.

There is question who this Sheshbazzar is, since the governor was also called Zerubbabel. Some conclude they are different names for the same man. Others conclude they are two men who worked together. There is evidence for both views. It is not clear which is correct.

Ezra Chapter 2

Names of Those Who Returned – Chapter 2

2:1-60 – *The people listed*

This chapter contains an enumeration of the people who returned according to their families. As described in chapter 1, they were among those who had been taken captive by Nebuchadnezzar, but were now allowed to return each to his own city.

These returned in the first group that returned in 536 BC, led by a group of men named here (compare the list in Neh. 7:7).

Jeshua most likely was the priest (probably the high priest) referred to in 3:2 and elsewhere in Ezra and Nehemiah.

Zerubbabel is also referred to frequently throughout these books (3:2,8; etc.). He evidently led this first group of captives who returned. He is listed in the lineage of Jesus (Matthew 1:12,13; Luke 8:27). This would indicate that he was a prince with right to the throne. However, the nation was led at this time, not by kings but by governors subject to the Persians. No king would reign as a legitimate descendant of David till Jesus became the spiritual King of the church.

There is some confusion regarding the name of his father: Shealtiel (Ezra 3:2 and the references above in Matthew and Luke) or Pedaiah (1 Chron. 3:19). A number of possible explanations exist (many people have more than one name, etc.), but these are not worth discussing in detail.

These verses record in detail the numbers of people from various cities, occupations, etc., who returned.

2:61-63 – *Priests not found in the genealogy were excluded from the priesthood.*

Certain men claimed they had a right to serve as priests, but they had no genealogy to prove their ancestry. Priests had to be descendants of Aaron (Numbers 16:39,40). Since there was no proof this was true in these men's case, they were excluded from being priests until such time as there was a priest who could consult Urim & Thummim to determine the legitimacy of their claims (Exodus 28:30).

Note that this was not meant as a conclusion that these men were evil sinners of some kind. They were still allowed to be part of God's people. The point is that they could not serve is special capacity as holders of office without having the required qualifications of that office. The same is true regarding men who seek to serve as elders and deacons today. The fact a man **lacks** evidence of qualification is sufficient basis to exclude him. We need not prove him guilty of evil.

2:64-70 – Tally of those who returned and of the contributions

The total number of people who returned was 42,360 who were reckoned as part of the congregation of Israel. Also there were 7337 who were servants that accompanied them (but apparently not of the lineage of the nation).

Also described are the number of animals they had and the amount of gold and silver that was contributed for the rebuilding of the temple.

All these people returned to the land of Israel and lived there in their cities.

Ezra Chapter 3

Laying of the Foundation of the Temple – Chapter 3

The Sacrificial Offerings Restored

3:1-3 – The altar was restored and sacrifices were offered.

The events here occurred in the "seventh month." Compare this to verse 6. This appears to mean the seventh month of the year, which would occur in the fall of the year. That would fit the events described, since several important acts of worship were commanded to occur in that month. Leviticus 23:23-44 says this included the Feast of Trumpets, the Day of Atonement, and the Feast of the Tabernacles (which is mentioned here in Ezra 3:4). [Compare Num. 29; Neh. 7:73; 8:1.]

The first group of exiles who returned were now settled in the land (2:70). Their first acts, even before they began work on the temple itself, were to restore the spiritual worship and praise of God. This is proper because, without proper honor to God they had no way to ask and receive His blessing on their efforts.

Jeshua and Zerubbabel led them in this work. Jeshua was the leader of the priests, presumably the High Priest (see 2:2; 3:8; Neh. 12:1,8). Zerubbabel led the government and appears to be the appointed governor (see also 2:2; 3:8; etc.).

They built the altar as a place to make their burnt offerings as the Law of Moses required. This is described in Deuteronomy 12:5,6 and many other passages. God had commanded that, when they entered the land, He would designate a place where they were supposed to worship Him and offer their sacrifices. This was done, of course, on an altar. Israel here erected an altar so they could have a place to offer sacrifices.

They did this though they feared the people of the land. We will see that the people were a real threat to them (chapter 4). Reinstituting the worship of God would likely alienate these people. But at the same time, they needed to worship God, and the altar gave them a means to request His care and protection against the people.

So they built the altar and began the regular offerings, including the morning and evening offerings. These were required every day of the week, as described in Numbers 28:2-8.

3:4-6 – The Feast of the Tabernacles and required sacrifices were observed.

They also kept the Feast of Tabernacles. This is mentioned in Leviticus 23:33-44 (Deuteronomy 16:13-17; compare Nehemiah 8:14ff). This feast required the people to build booths to dwell in for a period of seven days as a remembrance of their travels in the wilderness after God freed them from Egypt. Many offerings were associated with each day of the Feast of Tabernacles, as listed in Numbers 29:12-38. The returned exiles carefully observed these daily offerings.

And from that time on they offered all the regularly required sacrifices. These included the ones required at the beginning of each month (the New Moons – see Numbers 28:11-15). They also kept all the appointed feasts that God had commanded. 2 Chronicles 2:4.

All this began with the first day of the seventh month (see verse 1). The people willingly offered a freewill offering to the Lord (Numbers 29:39). And all this was done before they had even laid the foundation of the temple.

Likewise we, if we want God's blessings on our lives, must purify our worship and praise to Him. If we seek to restore our worship and service to Him, we must be sure we offer the honor that pleases Him.

The Foundation of the Temple Laid

3:7-9 – Work on the temple was begun.

The people then began the work of rebuilding the temple. They had to hire the workers (masons and carpenters) who had the required skills to do the work. They also had to purchase the necessary materials. They ordered cedar logs from Lebanon, and paid the people of Sidon and Tyre to bring them to the sea at the seaport of Joppa (see **map**). This would then require transporting them overland to Jerusalem. They paid for these provisions by sending food, drink, and oil. This is like what happened when Solomon built the first temple – 2 Chronicles 2:10,16; compare 2 Samuel 5:9-11. The funds for the work were apparently part of what King Cyrus had authorized in 1:2 (compare 6:3).

The work began in the second month of the second year after they had left Persia, at the direction of Zerubbabel, Jeshua (see verse 2) and the rest of the priests and Levites (compare 1 Chron. 23:24). The Levites, in particular, were the ones who oversaw the work, all of them from age twenty and up being involved. They, of course, were the tribe of the priests and, as such, they had been appointed as a tribe to care for the temple and the worship there.

In particular, the Levites were directed in this work by Jeshua, the High Priest, and others named Kadmiel and Henadad (along with their families), who were apparently among the Levites. Also included were some among Judah. I know nothing else about these specific men.

3:10,11 – When the foundation had been laid, the people worshiped God.

The building began, naturally, with the foundation. When this had been completed, a ceremony was conducted to praise God for the work accomplished thus far.

Priests were dressed in their priestly apparel having trumpets. Along with Levites, the sons of Asaph, they led the people in singing, praising God, and giving thanks to His name. This was done as had been ordained by King David (see 1 Chronicles 6:31ff; the sons of Asaph are specifically mentioned as being part of this work in 1 Chronicles 25:1ff).

They sang praise to God, giving thanks to Him for His goodness and mercy toward Israel. Then the people gave a great shout, praising God, because the foundation of the house was laid.

Note that the use of instrumental music (trumpets and cymbals) in worship is here, as elsewhere, expressly described and authorized in the **Old** Testament. If God still wants such instruments today, why are there no such passages in the **New** Testament that clearly describe them and authorize their use in our worship today? Instead, every New Testament passage says simply to sing (Ephesians 5:19; Colossians 3:16; etc.).

For further information, see our articles on instrumental music in worship at our Bible Instruction web site at www.gospelway.com/instruct/.

3:12,13 – While many people shouted in praise to God, older people who would seen the previous temple wept.

The people shouted in praise to God, but many of the older men who had seen the first temple, wept aloud when the foundation of this temple had been laid. So the weeping of the people mingled with the shouts of joy, and the noise could be heard from far away.

It is not clear whether the people who wept did so for joy or sorrow. It could be that the new temple did not compare in glory to the original one, yet that is not stated and would seem to be hard to tell just by looking at the foundation. (Haggai 2:3 refers to such an idea, however this came much later in the reign of Darius, and could well refer to the progress of the building after much more than just the foundation had been built.)

Often the greatest expression of joy is found, not in shouting aloud, but in weeping for joy. Those who were old enough to have seen the original temple, to have gone into captivity and suffered through it for many years, would surely be the ones most deeply moved now to return to Judah and see the new temple beginning construction. Tears of joy would surely be appropriate.

Another possibility is that the people wept in sorrow for the sin that had led to the destruction of the temple.

Note that it is good for God's people to praise Him and give Him honor and glory for any good we accomplish. Remember that it is His work being done through us. These people could never have built the temple had God not empowered it — they surely had been unable to do so for many years while in captivity. So we will accomplish good for God only with His blessings. Let us remember that we are able to do the work only because He blesses us, and that any good done is really a blessing He gives. So let us give Him glory.

Ezra Chapter 4

People of the Land Oppose the Work – Chapter 4

Whenever God's people do His work, there will always be adversaries. People will oppose the work and seek to prevent it or at least to so subvert it as to destroy its real intended effect. This is what happened with the Jews in their work of building the temple. Since we will experience similar problems, there are lessons we can learn from the tactics of God's enemies here and from the means used to deal with them.

4:1-3 - Religious Compromise

4:1,2 – People of the land sought to participate in the work, claiming they too were servants of the true God.

The first tactic of the adversaries was to try to become part of the group working on the temple. They claimed to be servants of the true God since the time they had been brought to the land by Esarhaddon, king of Assyria. So they wanted to be part of the work.

The record does not clearly state what their intent was. Perhaps they would have perverted the temple for their own purposes. Or maybe they intended to cause strife to hinder the work. Or perhaps they would have truly joined in the work, provided they would be permitted to continue their own perverted worship in the temple. In any case, we will see that they did not really want to truly serve God according to His true pattern.

Background of the people in the land

2 Kings 17:24-41 records how these people came to the land, and it explains why Zerubbabel was right to reject their help. When the Assyrians had removed the Israelites from the land, they had also

brought into the land people from other nations who were not Israelites either in lineage or in religion.

At first, these people did not worship the true God. They were eventually taught about God, and they did attempt to worship Him after a sort, but they also worshiped their false gods as they had in their homelands. We are expressly told that they continued in their false perverted form of worship, even as they professed to honor God. Hence, God rejected their worship. 2 Kings 17:32-34,41

4:3 – *The leaders of Israel refused to allow the people of the land to participate.*

Now in Zerubbabel's day, the people of the land came to help on the temple, but he rejected their help. He said the people of the land had no part in the matter, but the Jews would do the work by themselves. He pointed out that King Cyrus had authorized the work (1:1,2), so they were acting legitimately, both according to God's law and according to civil law.

To accept their help would have been to have religious fellowship with people in error. The worship offered by these people professed to honor God but was not according to God's authorized pattern. To accept their help on the basis of their claim that they worshiped God, would have been to declare them to be acceptable before God despite their error.

Modern applications

Likewise today, there are people who tell us they worship the true God - they don't openly profess to rebel against God - but they do not truly serve according to His prescribed authority. They may be members of some denomination, having never been truly converted, or they may serve God with unauthorized practices (Matthew 15:9,13; Galatians 1:8,9; 2 John 9-11; Colossians 3:17; Jeremiah 10:23; Proverbs 14:12; 3:5,6; Revelation 22:18,19; 1 Timothy 1:3; 2 Timothy 1:13).

We may be tempted to worship with them, or to use them in our worship services, or otherwise appear to fellowship them. Most denominations gladly welcome such people into their fellowship, and today many members of "churches of Christ" advocate fellowshipping such people. But we must refuse to fellowship such people today for the same reasons the Jews here refused to do so. If their worship and conduct is not according to God's word, then we sin if we fellowship them and we make it appear that their conduct is acceptable. (See 2 John 9-11; Ephesians 5:11; Proverbs 17:15; 2 Corinthians 6:17-7:1; 1 Timothy 5:22; Psalms 1:1,2; 1 Corinthians 15:33; Romans 1:32; Acts 7:58; 8:1; 22:20; etc.)

Note that, when we refuse, people will most likely accuse us of being in the wrong. As happened here, the people we refuse to accept may resent our action and become our adversaries. Or other people who hear about our stand may accuse us of being wrong. Some may accuse us of driving people away from the truth. In any case, when we take the stand taken by God's people here, we can be sure that some will accuse us of being in the wrong and will defend those who are perverting God's worship.

People today, who resent our refusal to fellowship religious error, should carefully consider passages such as this. And we should carefully consider it, when we are tempted to compromise with error and perversions of God's pattern.

4:4,5 - Harassment

4:4,5 – The people of the land tried to frustrate the work.

Having been forbidden a role in the work, the people of the land became a hindrance, trying to discourage the work. They made trouble and even hired people to try to frustrate the work. We are told some more about the methods that were used in the book of Nehemiah. These efforts continued until the times of king Darius.

The chronology of this chapter is confusing, because the names of the kings do not seem to fit the order of events. Perhaps the author, having introduced the fact the people tried to hinder the work, gives some examples from the reigns of later kings that did not follow chronologically but just illustrate the point, then later returns to the chronology.

The Waldron's argue that Ahasuerus (in verse 6) and Artaxerxes (in verse 7) are not the later leaders we commonly think of by those names (see introductory notes). They claim both these terms refer to Cambyses, who succeeded Cyrus (remember that kingdoms often have more than one king by the same name). However, they offer no proof. Such an explanation would make the chronology fit better, but why the name changes? Could it be that various Persian rulers were called by these names, just like various Egyptian rulers were called "Pharaoh," various Roman rulers called "Caesar," and various New Testament Jewish kings called "Herod"?

4:6-24 - False Accusation and Legal Opposition

4:6-10 – The people of the land wrote to the king making accusations against the Jews.

One method the people of the land attempted was to write a letter to the civil government and make false accusations against the Jews, hoping the authorities would stop the Jews' work. The letter was sent to the king of Persia and was written in the Aramaic language, since this presumably was the proper form of such an official appeal.

We are told here the names of various individuals who were behind the letter. Specifically, the men who wrote the letter were Rehum the commander and Shimshai the scribe. They were accompanied by various representatives of the nationalities of people who had been moved into the land. These groups are named in verse 9 (compare 2 Kings 17:24; Ezra 5:6; 6:6).

Verse 9 says that Osnapper had captured these people and settled them in the land. Presumably, this is just another name for the Assyrian king Esarhaddon (verse 2).

4:11-16 – The people's letter claimed that the Jews would rebel against the king.

The people wrote a letter to King Artaxerxes informing him that the Jews were building the city of Jerusalem, repairing the walls, etc., and that if they were allowed to succeed, they would end up rebelling against the rule of Persia. They pointed out that history showed the Jews had rebelled repeatedly (compare 2 Chronicles 26:13). So they claimed they would surely rebel again if they rebuilt the city.

They claimed further that the people would not pay taxes, and the king would end up having no power in the whole region. They said this, they claimed, because they were so loyal to the king that they didn't want him to be dishonored!

Of course, they said nothing about the fact they just did not want to see the Jews succeed. And the fact there was no evidence these people intended to do any such thing was apparently irrelevant to them. They hoped the king would overlook their lack of evidence and would just look up the past history of the Jews. They hoped this would be sufficient to convince him to punish the current generation!

Furthermore, they conveniently failed to mention that the Jews had been specifically authorized to do this work by King Cyrus (1:1,2). The decrees of Persian kings could not be changed, even by the king who made the decree, let alone by other kings (as shown in Daniel and in Esther). So, they did not want the king to research and find Cyrus' decree. They just wanted him to find the Jews' past history of rebellion!

Joseph Free points out that these communications to the king were written in Aramaic. Liberal scholars have denied that they are authentic because they say the form of Aramaic used here was too recent to date to the time of Ezra. However, Free points out that the Elephantine papyri include letters written in Aramaic by a colony of Jews at about the time of Ezra. The Aramaic is quite similar to that used in these letters recorded in the book of Ezra. So archaeology has proved that the criticisms of the Liberal scholars are invalid.

Other similar examples and modern applications

The same trick has been used against God's people repeatedly. People who oppose God's work misrepresent the motives, teaching, and work of God's people by telling lies and half-truths. They hope to discredit the work and turn people against it – especially civil authorities – hoping people will pressure God's people to stop.

This method was used in the first century when Jesus' enemies claimed He intended to literally tear down the temple and rebuild it in three days, that He taught people not to pay taxes to Caesar, that He would be a king in competition with Caesar, that He committed blasphemy, that he cast out demons by the power of Beelzebub, etc. All these were half-truths or outright lies intended to turn people against Him.

So today, one favorite trick of people who oppose the gospel is to use lies and half-truths to misrepresent the real beliefs and intentions of God's people. We are said to believe in "water salvation," that we can earn our salvation, are legalists, lack love, follow Alexander Campbell, are "anti's," don't believe in cooperation, don't believe in helping orphans, etc. As with the Jews in the story in Ezra, these are all either completely untrue or else half-truths that miss the real point of our beliefs. But by prejudicially describing our views, people hope to prejudice others against us.

In the case of the Jews, we will see that these deceitful methods were temporarily successful. We must make sure they do not succeed in our day.

4:17-22 – *The king responded that the work of rebuilding the city should cease.*

King Artaxerxes responded that he had searched the archives and found that the Jews had indeed been a rebellious people. He found that the kings of the Jews had at times been mighty rulers who ruled over all the provinces in the area and demanded tribute from them. This would have been true, for example, in the times of David and especially Solomon (1 Kings 4:21; 1 Chronicles 18:3). Perhaps his point was that, if the Jews would do this in time past, they might indeed rebel in his day, as their enemies accused. Instead of paying tribute to him, they might seek to rule the people around them and seek tribute for themselves.

So he agreed with the Jews' enemies and determined to forbid the Jews to proceed with their building. He told the people of the land to see to it that the Jews stopped. He concluded that he saw no reason to allow activities in his realm that would harm his authority as king.

4:23,24 – *As a result, the work on the temple ceased.*

Of course, the king had decided exactly what the Jews' enemies wanted. Not only did the Jews not have his permission to continue with the work, but the enemies had his authority to put a stop to the work. They were naturally quite zealous to do so, even by force of arms if necessary.

So the Jews did stop working until the second year of the reign of Darius. (Note the apparent historical conflict here. This places Artaxerxes as reigning before Darius. This demonstrates that there must be some confusion of names here – there must have been more than one ruler with these names or rulers who had more than one name, etc.)

Apparently, the Jews made no effort to contact the king and explain that their work had been authorized by decree of king Cyrus. Since the laws of Medes and Persians could not be changed (Daniel 6), it would appear that this could have been corrected.

So the Jews must have given up too easily. In any case, it is clear they quit when God did not want them to. We must take care lest we be discouraged in our stand for truth by the apparent power, influence, and successes of those who oppose our work for God.

We do not need human authority for our work for God. We ought to obey God, rather than man (Acts 5:29). Even if civil authorities did decree that we should not serve God, we should do His work anyway. But in many cases, civil rulers can be influenced to approve or accept our work for God, if we will at least try. In this case, the Jews apparently just gave up without trying. We will see that God was displeased with them, and He will likewise be displeased with us if we let people of the land influence us to neglect the work He commands us to do.

Ezra Chapter 5

Prophets Encourage the Work to Continue – Chapter 5

5:1 – Haggai and Zechariah prophesied to the people.

Sometime later, the prophets Haggai and Zechariah prophesied to the people and urged them to continue the work on the temple. Haggai's teaching is recorded in the book of Haggai (see Haggai 1:1ff), and Zechariah's is recorded in the book of Zechariah (see Zechariah 1:1ff).

Haggai 1 gives helpful additional information regarding the events recorded here in Ezra. Haggai 1:1 says his prophecies began in the second year of king Darius. This agrees with Ezra 4:24, which had told us that the work on the temple stopped until the second year of Darius. Waldron says this would have been sixteen years after they returned to Judah. So the work had evidently been neglected for quite some time.

The book of Zechariah adds little about the current situation, although he later gives some prophecies indicating God's determination to bless the people in their work. Most of his prophecies are symbolic, and many are predictions regarding Jesus and the coming New Testament.

Why the people had not been working

Haggai 1:1-11 also helps us understand why the work on the temple had stopped and what God's attitude was toward the people for their neglect of the work. In 1:2 the people said ***it is not time*** to build the Lord's house. They were neglecting and postponing the work.

But 1:4 says that they themselves were now dwelling in paneled houses. They had plenty of time to build their own houses, and even had made them quite nice. They had provided better homes even than just basic necessities. But they had allowed the temple of God to continue to dwell in ruins.

So the temple was neglected because the people thought they did not have the time or the means or the ability to build. But they had built more than adequately for themselves. They may have used the decree of the king as an excuse to stop working on the temple (Ezra 4:24). But this was, at least to some extent, an excuse. As discussed on Ezra 4, they should have obeyed God even if that required them to disobey civil rulers. But they even had the authority of Cyrus behind them, which we will see was enough to authorize them to continue the work, had they been willing to do so. The truth is that they just preferred to go about their own affairs and seek their own prosperity instead of working on the temple.

Haggai points out that the real problem was in them and their conduct: "Consider your ways" (1:5,7). Here is the real problem! The problem was not their circumstances: It was them! Instead of working on the temple, they had sought their own prosperity. But they had failed to really achieve even that, because God hindered them. 1:6 - They worked at providing food and clothing for themselves, but they found the results inadequate. It was like working to earn money, then storing the money in a bag with holes – it is just lost. The effort does not produce the intended benefits.

God said the reason they had so much trouble meeting their own needs was that He was working against them, because His house was still in ruins (1:9). He had called for droughts on all the produce of their land (1:10,11). So the solution was for them to go get the wood and build the temple, so He could be properly glorified (1:8). Then He would bless them.

Lessons for us

Wouldn't God have much the same to say to many members of many local congregations of His people today? How often do we see members of the church who have plenty of time to provide themselves with nice houses, clothes, cars, and plenty of food? They live beyond necessities to the point of luxuries.

Yet in so many cases we neglect the Lord's work. We may have built nice meetinghouses to assemble in; but remember the temple today is the church, and the work He wants in the church goes far beyond just assembling. He wants us to spread the gospel to every person in our community and then beyond into the whole world. How active are we in that work?

How many are saying, "It is not time to do that work." We don't have the time now, we don't have the money, we are too small, people are not interested in the gospel, etc., etc. We have excuse after excuse, but the real problem is the same as with the Jews. The problem is not our circumstances; the problem is us! We are just more committed to our own interests than we are to the work of the Lord!

God may or may not withhold physical blessings from us when we fail to work for Him, yet surely He will often withhold His spiritual blessings. If we seek to please Him, we too need to "consider our ways." We need to be about the work He has given us and not let the work be hindered because of opposition or just plain indifference!

5:2 – The people returned to work on the temple.

Stirred up by the prophets Haggai and Zechariah, the leaders of the people got to work and led the people to get back to work on the temple. The leaders led and the teachers taught, so the people went to work!

This is also described in Haggai 1:12-15. Zerubbabel and Joshua (compare 2:2) determined to lead the people to get back to work. Note that Haggai 1:1 calls Zerubbabel the governor of Judah. He was a civil leader, where Joshua was the high priest and the leader of spiritual worship. Together they again led the people back to work. This began in the sixth month of the second year of the reign of Darius.

As a result, God spoke through Haggai and assured the people that God was once again with them (1:13). They had repented of their neglect and had gone back to work, so once again they had His favor. Various passages in Haggai and Zechariah continue to assure them of God's favor.

Likewise, we need preachers, teachers, and elders like Haggai and Zechariah who see the real problem and will speak God's message and warn the people of the need to get to work! Sometimes people will be stirred up to get the job done if they have the leadership they need. With the effort of dedicated teachers, like Haggai and Zechariah, and the leadership of committed men, like Zerubbabel and Jeshua, God's people today may be stirred up to get to work. If we do, we can have confidence that God will also be with us and bless our work for Him.

5:3-5 – The governor questioned the Jews about their work.

The people were questioned about this work by Tattenai, the governor of the region, along with another man named Shethar Bozenai and other companions. Tattanai is called the governor of the region beyond the River – presumably this is the river Euphrates. So he was a higher authority than Zerubbabel. The latter was governor of Judah, but Tattenai was governor over the whole region. So he had a right to investigate.

He began by asking what authority the Jews had for their work: who commanded them to work on the temple. This was a legitimate question. In fact, it was the question that should have been asked and answered properly in chapter 4. We will see that these rulers are evidently not prejudiced against the work of the Jews. They are a different group of people from those who lived in the land and actively opposed the work of the Jews in chapter 4. These people have proper authority; and as good rulers, they simply wanted to know what the law was and apply it properly. So they asked what law or authority the Jews had.

The Jews also responded respectfully and wisely this time. They told the rulers who all their leaders were in the work. And, we will see from the later story, that they told them of the authority that had been given them by Cyrus.

The civil rulers determined to check the matter out to see whether or not the king had a record of the authorization that the Jews claimed to have received. But in the meanwhile, they decided not to stop the work until they had consulted with Darius. Obviously, these rulers, not being from among the people of the land, were not hostile as had been the people in chapter 4. But the passage also says this happened by the power of God. He worked with the Jews so the rulers were favorable.

All this also shows that the Jews had been without excuse for stopping work in the first place. Had they told about the authority they had, and had they been determined to continue the work, God would have blessed them before so they never would have stopped the work. The fact He was displeased with them shows they should have continued working all along.

5:6-10 – The governor determined to write to King Darius.

These verses then record the letter Tattenai the governor, along with Shethar Boznai and his companions, sent to King Darius to inquire about the Jews' work on the temple. They began by explaining that the people of Judea were building a temple to their great God, making it of timber and heavy stones. They said the people were diligent in the work and the work was prospering.

They then told the king about their inquiry as to what authority they had to build the temple, and they had asked the names of the chief men among them. All this was being reported to the king, and it was an accurate record of what had happened.

According to Holden and Geisler, the reign of Darius is well known in history. The Behistun Relief pictures him and his soldiers leading defeated enemies by a rope. (page 280)

5:11-16 – The Jews responded that King Cyrus had authorized them to rebuild their temple.

This part of the letter then records the response the Jews gave to the rulers, including more detail than had been recorded in verse 4. The Jews had first said that they were servants of the great God who ruled heaven and earth, and the temple they were rebuilding had originally been built by one of their earlier great kings. This, of course, was a reference to Solomon, who had built the original temple (1 Kings 6:1,38).

The Jews then explained that their ancestors had later become unfaithful to God, so He had punished them by allowing the Babylonians to take them away into captivity (2 Chron. 36:16,17). At that time the temple had been destroyed by Nebuchadnezzar.

They then explained that, when King Cyrus of the Persians had come into power, he had decreed that they could return to Judea and rebuild the temple (see on 1:1). And in fact, he had returned to them the articles of gold and silver that Nebuchadnezzar had taken from the temple when he had destroyed it. All these had been given to a man named Sheshbazzar, who had been named governor and who had been commanded to bring these articles to Judea (1:7-11). This man had brought the articles as commanded and had begun building the foundation. But the temple had not been completed. Of course, the point was that they were now finishing what Cyrus had authorized many years before.

This was the reply that the Jews should have given in chapter 4 to the people of the land who stopped them from their work. If they had then the same commitment to the work that they had here in chapter 5, they would never have stopped the work. And that is why God was upset with them. Fortunately, they were now back on the job, and they have given a proper explanation to these rulers. And the rulers have given an accurate explanation of the matter to the king.

5:17 – The governor asked the king to search the archives and give a ruling in the matter.

Tattenai's letter to Darius accurately conveyed the situation as it was. Tattenai then requested that the king check this out in the records to see if Cyrus really had made such a decree as the Jews claimed. Then he asked the king to write back and tell the governor what the facts were and how he wanted them to handle this matter. The results will be recorded in the next chapter.

Note that this demonstrates an important Bible principle: God's people should submit to civil law, but it is Scriptural for us to appeal to the authority of human rulers to protect us from enemies and wrongdoers. Civil rulers are ordained of God for the punishment of evildoers and the reward of those who do good (Romans 13:1-7; 1 Peter 2:11-15). If that is their purpose, then God approves of our calling upon these rulers to protect our righteous cause. Paul used this principle several times when he was threatened with harm by those who opposed his work (Acts 22:25-29; 25:10-12).

Ezra Chapter 6

The Temple Completed – Chapter 6

6:1-5 – King Darius found the decree of Cyrus that authorized the Jews to rebuild the temple.

As the governor Tattenai had requested in his letter in chapter 5, King Darius made a search for the decree that the Jews claimed authorized their work. He searched in the archives where treasures were stored, and the decree was found recorded on a scroll in the palace in Achmetha in the province of Media. The NKJV footnote suggests that this was Ecbatana, capital of Media.

The decree said that Cyrus authorized the building of the temple, just as the Jews claimed, and as recorded already in Ezra 1:1-8; 5:13,14. It said the house of the Lord, where sacrifices were offered, should be rebuilt. The record even gave more detail than in Ezra 1. It said the height would be sixty cubits and the width sixty cubits (ninety feet by ninety feet). It would be built from three rows of heavy stones and one row of timber. This was the same as the original temple (1 Kings 6:36).

Furthermore, it said the expenses were to be paid from the treasury of the king (compare 3:7). And just as chapter 1 recorded, the gold and silver articles taken from the temple by Nebuchadnezzar should be returned to the house of God.

Verses 2-5 appear to be a record of the original decree written by Cyrus. But it also appears that the quotation begins the letter of King Darius to Tattenai, in response to the letter the governor had sent to the king. So that verses 6ff simply continue the king's response.

6:6-8 – Darius decreed that the work should be allowed to continue and even supported at government expense.

Having quoted the original decree, King Darius then continued by commanding governor Tattenai and his companions (compare 5:3,6) to stay far away from the Jews and not hinder the work on the temple in any way. They were to allow the governor and elders of the Jews to proceed with the work of building the house of God.

In fact, he commanded that the government should provide things needed for the work. Tax money should pay for the work and should be given to the men in charge of the work, so they work would not be hindered in any way.

6:9-12 – *Provisions were given for the work, and anyone who altered the edict would be cursed.*

Further, the king decreed that tax funds should be used to pay for the animals and other provisions to be used for the sacrifices that the priests needed day by day in the offerings to be made at the temple in Jerusalem. This would result in a sweet aroma to go up to the God of heaven.

I don't know that this means the king was converted to believing in the God of the Old Testament as the one true God. I suspect more likely he just wanted the blessing of all the gods in the empire, so he tried to please them all.

Further, he hoped the people would pray to God on behalf of the king and his sons. The New Testament likewise teaches that we should do the same for rulers today – 1 Timothy 2:1,2.

Then he went still further and proclaimed a severe curse on anyone who attempted to change his decree. He said that, for such a person, a timber should be removed from his own house and used to hang the man on. Then his house should be destroyed to the level of a refuse heap (compare Daniel 2:5; 3:29).

Finally, he called upon the God who caused His name to dwell in that place (Deuteronomy 12:5,11; 1 Kings 9:3) to destroy any person or king who sought to alter the decree or to destroy the temple that would be built in Jerusalem.

This was Darius' decree, and he commanded diligent obedience to it.

6:13-15 – *The people continued work on the temple till it was completed.*

Tattenai and his companions then proceeded to diligently do as the king commanded. The work on the temple proceeded and prospered, guided by the prophesying of Haggai and Zechariah (5:1).

The work thus proceeded till the temple was finished on the third day of the month Adar in the sixth year of Darius' reign. Haggai 1:1 said the work began again in the second year of Darius' reign (compare Ezra 4:24; 5:1), so it took approximately four years after the work began again till it was completed.

This was said to be done according to the command of Cyrus and Darius and Artaxerxes. The first two we have plainly seen were involved, but the involvement of Artaxerxes is less obvious. He became involved later (compare 7:1,11; Nehemiah 2:1), so perhaps this is included by looking forward to what he later did.

6:16-18 – With many sacrifices the people dedicated the temple and organized the priesthood.

Following the completion of the temple, a dedication ceremony was held. Solomon had conducted a similar ceremony when he originally built the temple (1 Kings 8:63; 2 Chronicles 7:5). This celebration occurred with great joy among the people and involved the offering of many sacrifices in the new temple: one hundred bulls, two hundred rams, four hundred lambs, and twelve male goats as a sin offering, one goat for each of the tribes of Israel.

Then the service of the temple was organized, including priests and Levites set up in their divisions as provided for in the law. See 1 Chronicles 23:6; 24:1; 2 Chronicles 35:5; Numbers 3:6; 8:9. These, of course, were the people that God had assigned to care for the tabernacle/temple and to offer the sacrifices there.

6:19-22 – The people then celebrated the Passover.

Now that the temple had been set up, the people were finally again able to participate in the various worship activities, including feast days, as provided for in the law. The temple had been completed in the month Adar, the last month of the Jewish religious calendar (according to Waldron). The next month would be the first month, which was when the Passover was to be celebrated. So the temple was completed just in time for the Passover.

The Passover was the annual memorial to the last plague God brought through Moses on the Egyptians. The firstborn son in each home of the Egyptians died; but God protected the children of the Israelites, if they placed the blood of the Passover lamb on their doors. It was celebrated each year on the 14th day of the first month, followed by the seven-day feast of Unleavened Bread. See Exodus 12:6,15; 13:6,7; 2 Chronicles 35:11; 30:21; 35:17.

The Jews kept this feast in the rebuilt temple, led by the priests and Levites. To do this the priests and Levites had to purify themselves, so they were ceremonially clean as required by the law. See 2 Chronicles 29:34; 30:15. The priests led in offering the required sacrifices for themselves, for the Levites, and for the people.

The Israelites who had returned from captivity ate the Passover along with those who had cleansed themselves from the defilement of the land so they could seek God (compare Ezra 9:11). These were apparently people from the region who had determined to follow God, along with those who returned from captivity.

The people also kept the seven days of the feast of unleavened bread. All this was done with joy, for the people rejoiced that God had returned them to the land by means of the decrees of the king of Assyria. Why refer to the king as the king of Assyria, rather than the king of Persia? Waldron claims that Darius was first king of Assyria as part of the Persian Empire. Then he became king also of the whole empire.

The principle of restoration

Note that we have here an example of the principle of restoration according to divinely revealed pattern in the written word. The priests were organized "as it is written in the Book of Moses" (verse 18). See also 3:1-6, especially verse 2. The law also spoke of the Passover. The people were able to know what to do to worship and serve God simply by reading and following the written word. This was true even though they had been gone for decades and neither the temple ritual nor the priesthood had been active for all those years. Likewise, we today can restore our service to God in His church by simply studying and following the written word of the gospel, even if people have not followed it for years.

Note also that this was done with great ***joy***. We ought to have great joy to see God's service restored in our own lives or in the lives of others where it has not been done (compare Luke 15). But too often we lose the joy until God's blessings are removed. Why provoke God to wrath, as Israel had done, till He punishes us so severely? Why not see all His great gifts to us day by day so that we rejoice at every opportunity to praise Him? Why be so unappreciative, as many are, so we do not have joy in our day-to-day service? Why wait till the opportunity is taken from us before we realize what we should have been doing?

Waldron points out that the story of Esther would have taken place during the reign of Xerxes (Ahasuerus) between Ezra 6 and 7.

Part 2: Spiritual Restoration of the People – Chapter 7-10

Ezra Chapter 7

Ezra Decreed to Lead Another Group to Return (458 BC) – Chapter 7

7:1-6 – *Ezra is introduced to the story as a skilled scribe in the Law of Moses.*

In this chapter we are introduced to Ezra himself. The previous chapters, though included in the book of Ezra, nevertheless happened several years before Ezra was personally involved in the events. The first group returned from Babylonian captivity in about 536 B.C. led by Zerubbabel, whom we have read about in chapters 1-6. Ezra led a group that returned in about 458 B.C., almost eighty years later. Many things can change in eighty years (compare the changes that have occurred in America in the last eighty years).

These things happened in the reign of Artaxerxes (verse 1). Compare Nehemiah 2:1. This was the son of the Xerxes who ruled during Esther's day.

We are given Ezra's lineage. To those of us under the New Testament, genealogies are of little value. But to a Jew under the Old Testament, ancestry was very important. This was especially true in Ezra's case, because his lineage showed him to be a descendant of

Aaron (verse 5). This qualified him to be a priest, as he is referred to several times in the book.

We are told some things about Ezra's character. He was a skilled scribe in the Law of Moses – compare 7:11,12,21. Scribes were men whose job was to make records and keep accounts and make copies of records, etc. But Ezra was a scribe especially of the Law of Moses; such scribes would copy and study copies of the Scriptures. They did not have modern printing equipment, so each copy of each book had to be made by hand. In doing this work, scribes often gained a good knowledge of the books.

We are also told that the hand of the Lord His God was upon Ezra. He clearly was a good man who lived close to God and was devout. As a result God blessed him to fulfill his requests from the king as described in the following verses.

The Law of Moses and the Law of God

Note that the Law of Moses is said to be that which the Lord God of Israel had given. Some people try to distinguish the Law of Moses from the Law of God as two separate laws. Seventh Day Adventists and others say the Law of God was the 10 Commands and was never removed by Jesus so is still in effect today. They say the Law of Moses was the rest of the Old Testament (other than the 10 Commands) and is what Jesus removed on the cross.

However, this passage says Ezra was a scribe of the Law of Moses, which God gave. That would imply that the Law of Moses is the Law of God. Verse 12 then settles the matter for sure, saying that Ezra was a scribe of the Law of God. Verse 11 says he was expert in the words of the commands of the Lord. So there is no difference between the Law of God and the Law of Moses.

For further information, see our articles on the old law for today at our Bible Instruction web site at www.gospelway.com/instruct/.

7:7-9 – Ezra led a group of Jews from Babylon to Jerusalem.

Here is a brief summary of Ezra's trip. He left Babylon on the first day of the first month of the seventh year of Artaxerxes' reign, and he arrived in Jerusalem four months later on the first day of the fifth month. With him were priests, Levites, and people of various other occupations.

The Nethinim are mentioned in 2:43; 8:20; 1 Chronicles 9:2. *International Standard Bible Encyclopedia* says these were servants in the temple, but their history and origin are uncertain. Note especially that Ezra 8:20 says that David appointed them to help the Levites in the temple service.

Note that this is just a brief overview of what we will read about in detail in the following verses — we do not have two separate trips led by Ezra. (Compare Genesis 1 to Genesis 2).

7:11 – Ezra prepared his heart to seek the law of the Lord, to do it, and to teach it.

Here we are told more about Ezra's character. Four important steps are described regarding Ezra's attitude toward the law, all of which we should imitate.

(1) He prepared his heart.

To be acceptable, all service to God must come from the heart (Romans 6:17; Matthew 15:16ff; Proverbs 4:23; etc.) We will never properly learn God's will, let alone do it and teach others, until we get our own hearts right (Acts 17:11).

(2) He then sought the law of the Lord.

We can never do God's will till we know it. The NKJV footnote on "sought" says "study." We must be diligent students if we are to know God's law (Psalms 1:1; 119:47,48,97-99; 19:7-11; Acts 17:11; Joshua 1:8; Deuteronomy 6:6ff; John 8:32; Hosea 4:6; Hebrews 5:12; 1 Peter 2:2; 2 Timothy 2:15; Proverbs 2:1-20; Matthew 5:6). So Ezra's proper attitude of heart led him to study to learn God's law.

As a result of this study, he became expert in the law (verse 11). Some want to ridicule us if we think we need to be experts in God's law, but surely it is as valuable for us as it was for Ezra. Compare Psalms 119:45.

(3) He then practiced what he learned.

Knowledge is worthless without application (Matthew 7:21-27; 22:36-39; John 14:15,21-24; Acts 10:34,35; Romans 2:6-10; 6:17,18; Hebrews 5:9; 10:39; 11:8,30; Galatians 5:6; 2 Thessalonians 1:8,9; James 1:21-25; 2:14-26; Luke 6:46; 1 Peter 1:22,23; 1 John 5:3; 2:3-6). Many people know what God expects but don't practice it. Ezra was not one of these.

(4) He then taught others what he himself had learned.

See Deuteronomy 33:10; Nehemiah 8:1-8. You cannot teach what you do not know, and you will never teach effectively what you do not practice (Hebrews 5:12ff; Romans 2:21ff; 1 Timothy 4:16). We today are obligated to obey God and to be teachers to the extent of our ability (Acts 8:1,4; Galatians 6:1; 2 Timothy 2:2,24-26; Hebrews 3:12-14; 5:12-14; 10:24; James 5:19,20; 1 Peter 3:15). The steps Ezra followed are the right steps in the right order. We would do well to imitate him.

7:11-18 – Artaxerxes wrote a letter authorizing Ezra to lead people to Jerusalem and make necessary provisions.

Here is the beginning of the decree Artaxerxes made authorizing Ezra to lead people to Judah. He began by addressing Ezra as a scribe of the law of God. Artaxerxes decreed that Ezra could go to Jerusalem and take with him all Israelites, including priests and Levites, who voluntarily chose to go.

He was to go to see how the people in Jerusalem and Judah fared as regards their obedience to the law of God. And he was authorized to take with him silver and gold from the king and his advisors as an offering to God. Also, the people could send free-will offerings for the service in the temple. These should be used to buy animals and other substances for offerings. The rest of the silver and gold could be used according to the best judgment of Ezra and the people as needed according to God's will.

7:19-23 – Ezra was authorized to arrange what was needed for service in the temple.

They also could take articles that could be used in the temple. Then the king issued a decree to those beyond the River who were in charge of the king's treasure to give whatever Ezra requested up to one hundred talents of silver, one hundred kors of wheat, one hundred baths of wine, one hundred baths of oil, and salt without prescribed limit. Other things needed for the temple could be bought or provided from these gifts.

They were to have whatever they needed to do God's will in the temple. The king was concerned to please God, so as to avoid bringing wrath on his realm because of displeasing God. (It does not seem that this proves Artaxerxes was converted completely to God's service. Perhaps he just viewed God as A god who truly was powerful and did not want to bring the disfavor of that god.)

7:24-26 – Religious leaders were not to be taxed, and judges should enforce the laws.

The king then decreed that those who served in the temple should not have to pay any form of taxes (see verse 7 regarding Nethinim). And he authorized Ezra to set up judges and other rulers to make sure God's law was properly enforced. This required judges to know God's law, and Ezra was to teach it to those who did not know it (it could also be that he was to teach the people the law – 2 Chronicles 17:7; Malachi 2:7). Compare Exodus 18:21,22; Deuteronomy 16:18.

Those who would not obey the law were to be punished by whatever means was deemed best: death, banishment, confiscation of goods (as in a fine), or imprisonment. Note that laws must be enforced to be effective, and people must know the laws in order to be able to obey them. The duty of rulers is to teach people the law and to punish those who disobey. We today need judges who will diligently follow this pattern.

7:27,28 – Ezra thanked God for the king's decree.

For this decree of the king, Ezra praised God. He could improve the service in the temple and make the temple more attractive. He considered this to be a blessing from God. The king made the decree, but Ezra gave glory to God for moving the king to do so. We should give thanks to God for our blessings, even when they come through people.

So Ezra began to prepare for the journey by finding leaders of the Israelites to make the journey with him.

Ezra Chapter 8

Preparation and Journey Led by Ezra – Chapter 8

In chapter 7, King Artaxerxes had authorized Ezra to lead another group of exiles to return to Judea. This chapter gives the details of that group and its return (whereas chapter 7 had simply summarized the fact that it was done).

8:1-14 – *The list of people to return with Ezra*

These verses give a list of the names of the leaders of the people who made the trip with Ezra. Note the reference to "with me" in verse 1, showing this was the group that Ezra had been authorized to lead.

The number of men (not counting families) that returned with Ezra was 1354 (including the Levites, etc., added in verses 15ff). This was a much smaller group than the first group that Zerubbabel had led, which had totaled over 50,000 (compare chapter 2).

8:15-20 – *Levites were found to accompany the group.*

The people who had volunteered to make the trip were gathered together by the river Ahava (compare verses 21,31). They camped there three days, but when Ezra searched among them he found no Levites. Apparently there were priests, but the Levites were responsible to assist the priests in the temple. So the lack of Levites was a problem.

Ezra discussed this with the leading men ("chief men" – ASV) and the men of understanding ("teachers" – ASV). He gave them a command to carry to a man named Iddo, who was a chief man at a place called Casiphia. Iddo was a leader of the Nethinim, so he was instructed to bring servants for the house of God. See verse 20 below regarding Nethinim.

The instruction to Iddo resulted in a group of men to return to Jerusalem to do the needed work of service. A man of understanding named Sherebiah, of the tribe of Levi, came with his sons and brothers. Also other Levites came, so the total Levites were 38.

Also 220 Nethinim came, itemized by name. Here we have an explanation as detailed as any of who the Nethinim were. They are said to be people appointed by David and other leaders to serve the Levites. So the Levites helped the priests in the temple, and the Nethinim helped the Levites. Compare 2:43; 7:7.

Note that Ezra gave the credit to God for these men. He and others had worked to bring it about, but God blessed their effort. We should remember to also give God credit and thanks when our needs are met.

8:21-23 – *The people asked God to bless and protect them on their journey.*

Before beginning the journey, the people made special request of God by means of fasting for His aid and protection. Ezra had told the king that God was with those who served Him and against those who did not (see 7:6,9,28; Josh. 23:16). So he did not think it would be fitting now to turn and ask the king for armed guards to protect them. Instead, they made request of the Lord and put their faith in Him. This request was answered as they did arrive safely.

One reason why they needed protection is described in the following verses. They had much silver and gold and other valuables with them to take to the work in the temple. This might endanger them from robbers, etc. But God cared for them and they had no such problems.

Surely we also need to ask God's blessings on the work we do. We should request His care and protection when we travel, or when we undertake any work for Him. If the Lord does not bless our work, we will not accomplish good for Him. If His blessing is on the work, then we can accomplish much.

Note that this passage clearly illustrates the Biblical purpose of fasting. We are expressly told that they fasted and prayed in order to entreat God. This was a means of showing how seriously and sincerely they sought God's blessings on their work. See also 1 Samuel 7:6; 2 Chronicles 20:3.

Note also that, when we make a request of God and then receive what we asked for, we can and should give God credit that He answered our prayer.

8:24-30 – *Men were appointed to be responsible for the treasure.*

The king had authorized people to make free-will offerings for the work of the temple, and the king and his counselors had also made donations – 7:14-16. This resulted in a great quantity of valuables being transported with Ezra's group. There were six hundred and fifty talents of silver, silver articles {weighing} one hundred talents, one hundred talents of gold, twenty gold basins worth a thousand drachmas, and two vessels of fine polished bronze, precious as gold. Compare the amount of the first group recorded in 1:9-11.

Preparation for the trip required making individuals responsible for caring for the precious things being taken. This was not left up to everybody in general but nobody in particular. Ezra made twelve specific individuals responsible for various items. The quantity was measured to them to keep, so it could be measured again to be sure they delivered the complete amount when they arrived in Jerusalem.

Note how this illustrates the concept of stewardship. These men were in charge of something that did not belong to them; in fact, it belonged to God's work. They were in charge of it, but could not do with it just whatever they chose. They were to care for it and use it properly, but then they were to give account for what they did with it.

Ezra said that these men were holy or set apart to do this work. They were caring for holy possessions for the temple, so they were to be holy in their work. Compare Leviticus 21:6-8; 22:2,3.

We today support God's work by freewill offerings on the first day of the week (1 Corinthians 16:1,2). Like the funds here in Ezra, these funds today are given to specifically do God's work in the spiritual temple, the church. That makes them holy, or set apart to God. They can no longer be used for just anything we desire or anything men may choose. They must be used according to God's plan, and to use them for other things would be to misuse that which is holy.

We also have God's holy word and the duties of His church. These are holy responsibilities also to care for, so we too must be holy people to do them (1 Peter 1:15ff; 2:5-10). In a sense, our responsibility is even greater than that of these men. They were stewards of only material wealth. We are stewards of that which leads to eternal life. Someday we will be called to account for how we used these gifts. Are we using them wisely?

Then note that Ezra and the people had prayed to God for protection. But having prayed, they also took measures to do what they could to bring about what they prayed for. They asked God's protection, but then appointed men to be specifically responsible to protect the valuables. Likewise, we pray for daily bread, for the gospel to be spread, for wisdom, etc., but then we must work to the extent we are able to bring about what we prayed for. God deserves the credit, but He expects us to do what we can.

8:31-34 – *The journey was completed and the people arrived safely in Jerusalem.*

The people, having completed their preparations, began their journey on the 12th day of the first month. 7:8,9 had said that they began on the first day of the first month. I assume this means that was when they gathered to begin the journey, but the preparations described here took the intervening time. So they actually left on the twelfth day.

God answered their prayer for protection, so they arrived safely with no ambushes from enemies. Note again the credit is given to God for the blessing of safety.

Having arrived safely in Jerusalem, they waited there for three days. Then the men who had been entrusted with the valuables delivered them to those in charge of the temple. The implication is that, when the goods were measured, all was found to be present. Note that the stewards were called to account for their stewardship. It is proper to check up on those who are stewards. They should be glad to provide things honorable in the sight of men as well as God – 2 Cor. 8:21.

8:35,36 – *The people offered sacrifice to God and delivered the king's decree.*

The people then made sacrifice of praise to God. This was done by those who had returned from captivity. I assume that means all who had returned, including people of both groups. The many animals offered are described.

The people also went to the governing authorities of the region to deliver to them the decree from the king (see chapter 7). This resulted in their receiving the finances and cooperation that the king had decreed.

So the second group had arrived safely from their journey.

Ezra Chapter 9

The People Put Away Foreign Wives and Children - Chapter 9,10

The Sin of Intermarriage Is Discovered

9:1,2 – Ezra learned that many of the Jews had intermarried with people of the land.

Ezra had brought the group of exiles back in chapter 8, and the first thing that is recorded as happening was a major problem. So often, when we rejoice in having received a great blessing or achieved a good work, the devil soon seeks to defeat or discourage us by problems.

The law had required that the people of Israel were not to marry the people of the nations that they were to defeat and remove from the land (the nations listed in verse 1). The purpose of this was to keep their evil influence from leading the Israelites to sin especially in idolatry (see verse 12; Deuteronomy 7:1-5; Exodus 23:32; 34:12-16; Leviticus 18:24-30; Joshua 23:12,13; Nehemiah 13:23-27). However, the people in Judah had committed this sin, and the leaders and rulers of the people had been the most guilty.

Sin is always tragic. Serious consequences so often follow. This is true of all sins, even sins by those who make no claim to be God's people. But sin is especially tragic when it is committed by the people of God, because they are the ones who have professed allegiance to God and who therefore ought to be most faithful. Worst of all is when the leaders of God's people are involved. When the leaders go astray, they often lead the other people astray, setting a bad example, and failing to demand purity of the people. Elders, preachers, teachers, and mature Christians need to learn this lesson. See Acts 20:28-30; 1 Timothy 4:12; 1 Peter 5:1-3.

The New Testament does not contain a direct and express prohibition against marriage to people who are not Christians, like the Old Testament passages listed above (though some believe there are indirect prohibitions of it). But the practice ought to be avoided today, because it often leads to consequences exactly like these Old Testament passages warn against.

Furthermore, there are many problems, dangers, and temptations to one who marries a non-Christian. There may be conflicts over how to raise the kids, how much to give to the church, whether or not to attend all the services or whether to attend a denomination, what moral standards we will follow, who our closest friends will be, even where we will live (in a town with no faithful church?), etc.

And even if there is no direct conflict in these matters, still the one who is not a Christian does not share that which is most important in life to the Christian – a relationship with God. The Christian must live with the daily knowledge that the dearest person on earth to him/her is destined for eternal punishment, and the non-Christian's example works against the Christian in raising the children and teaching the lost, etc. Surely we can see that a Christian would be foolish to put himself in such a situation, yet it happens time and time again.

9:3,4 – *The righteous people grieved over the sin.*

Ezra was deeply grieved over this sin by the people. He tore his clothes and plucked out some of his hair and beard. These were signs of great grief. All others who respected God's words came together with him to grieve. They are said to tremble at the word of God – compare Isaiah 66:2; Ezra 10:3. They realized the severe consequences of disobedience to God.

People who are aware of the sins committed by others ought to feel great grief. It is right that we should grieve over sin. Sin is terrible in what it does to our lives, our eternal destinies, and especially our relationship to God. People who do not grieve over sin are people who are not likely to live apart from sin.

This sin in particular brought grave consequences in this life, even if people are willing to repent of it, as we will see. We will also see that the sin of unscriptural divorce and remarriage today likewise brings grave consequences. The situation is tragic in that the people involved are going to suffer greatly for their sin either in this life or in eternity (or both). It is truly a cause for grief.

9:5-9 – *Ezra began confession by praising God for his blessings to the people.*

Not only had Ezra torn his clothing and plucked out hair, but he had also been fasting. Fasting is a way of showing grief. It is also a way, when accompanied by prayer, of making especially serious requests to God and showing extreme sorrow for sin (compare 10:6).

At the time of the evening sacrifice, Ezra went to God in prayer over this matter. It is always right to go to God in prayer about our problems, especially spiritual problems and times of great spiritual needs. Those who care about God's will, and who therefore grieve over sin, will naturally be driven to prayer when they see sins, especially such grave ones affecting so many people as in this case. And those who commit the sin must pray to God to be forgiven (Acts 8:22; Matthew 6:12; 21:28-32; 2 Corinthians 7:10; 1 John 1:8-10; Proverbs 28:13).

Ezra deeply expressed his grief in prayer (compare Daniel 9:7,8). He fell to his knees, spread out his hands toward God, and was too ashamed to even lift his face to God. The people were so guilty He could not face God. He said their sins had covered their heads and risen to the heavens (Psalms 38:4; 2 Chronicles 28:9).

Ezra recalled that which God obviously knew – that the nation had frequently sinned against God, and for those sins God had sent them into captivity (Psalms 106:6; 2 Chronicles 36:14-17; Daniel 9:5,6). Even the kings and priests had been sent to the sword (death), plunder, captivity, and humiliation. You would think they would have learned the lesson to avoid sin.

Now, by God's grace they had just been allowed to return from captivity. Ezra had just led a group of exiles back from captivity. This was a revival granted by God's mercy through the Persians. God had allowed them to return to rebuild the temple and the city wall (as in the book of Nehemiah).

Yet for all these punishments and mercies, here they are in sin again! Though they had been slaves, God had not forsaken them. Surely they ought to have known better than to turn around and go right back into the kind of sin that led to idolatry and led to captivity.

How many times are Christians today likewise guilty? We too are all sinners saved by the grace of God. We deserve to be punished eternally for our sins, just as Israel deserved captivity. Yet by His great mercy God sent Jesus to die for us and offer us the hope of eternal life, which we surely do not deserve. Yet how often do we just go right back into sin, even sometimes knowing we should not do so?

Note that Ezra refers to those who had returned as a "remnant" (v8; compare verse 15). A remnant is a small part that somehow has been left over from some larger substance. In this case, the greater part of Israel had been destroyed for sin and remained in captivity. Those who returned were a small part of the group. This concept of a remnant is common in Biblical teaching to refer to the small part of those who maintain a relationship with God (compare Romans 9:27). Yet in this case, a major part even of the remnant had sinned. How tragic!

9:10-15 – *Ezra confessed to God the people's guilt.*

But for all God's goodness in returning the people from captivity, now they again had forsaken His commands. Specifically, God had warned them that the land was unclean, having been defiled by the sins of the people, especially idolatry. Therefore, He had commanded them to separate themselves from the people of the land so as to avoid their sins. Yet Israel had again committed sin; instead of separating themselves from the people, they had intermarried with then. God had expressly forbidden this because of the iniquities and abominations of the people of the land (see references on verse 2). Had they maintained separation and purity, God would have kept them in the land to receive its great blessings even for future generations. But they had been cast out of the land because of sin.

After all that God had done to punish the people for their previous sins, and then delivered them from that punishment, you would surely think the people would know better than to go back into sin now. How could they so presume on His mercy? Did they think he would spare them now? Ezra affirms that surely such sin would lead God to be so angry He would consume them and this time leave no remnant.

Note that Ezra says God punished them less than they deserved (verse 13; compare Psalms 103:10). This is a description of grace. Grace leads God to offer us salvation and forgiveness despite the fact we deserve punishment. Hence, it is unmerited or undeserved favor. What we deserve is punishment.

And then note again the reference to the returned exile as a "remnant" (verses 14,15; see notes on verse 8).

Ezra Chapter 10

The Sin Resolved

10:1-4 – The people proposed to make a covenant requiring that unscriptural wives be given up.

In chapter 9, the returned exiles had discovered a serious spiritual problem in their midst. Many men, including many leaders of the nation, had married wives of foreign nations in disobedience to the law. Ezra had mourned for the sin and prayed to God at length confessing the people's evil. As Ezra continued in this prayer, a large group of people assembled and joined him in grieving for the sin, weeping bitterly.

This chapter describes the solution to the problem that was determined and, in so doing, shows us important principles about removing sin from God's people and spiritual restoration of those who have departed from God's way. In particular, it shows us what needs to be done when people have committed the sin of entering into sinful marriages, which they have no right to enter.

The solution was proposed by a man named Shechaniah. Nothing else is known about this man, but he was a wise and courageous man to propose the solution. First, he acknowledged what had been done and that it was a sin: men had married people from the surrounding forbidden nations (see notes on 9:2 for Scriptures and details regarding this sin). Yet he said there was hope. Even in time of the deepest sin, there is hope if people are willing to turn from it.

He said the people who were guilty needed to repent, and the only way to overcome the harm done and do proper restitution was to put away the foreign wives and their children. He proposed that they make a covenant with God to do this. This would be done according to the law and according to the guidance of those who tremble at God's law (see 9:4).

Note that repentance required giving up the wives, since the marriages themselves were illegitimate. They could not continue in the marriages, because they had no right to be in them. They were forbidden because the foreign wives would influence the men of Israel to worship idols and commit other pagan sins. So long as the marriages continued, the sin would continue. So the only solution was to get out of the marriages.

This was done by means of a covenant before God - a solemn promise and commitment before Him (compare 2 Chronicles 34:31). The putting away was done by a commitment made before God and before the leaders of God's people. Of course, the men involved had to follow through and cease living with those wives.

Similar repentance is required today.

The Bible demands repentance as a condition for forgiveness today, even as it did then, whether the sin was committed before conversion or afterward (Luke 13:3,5; 24:47; Acts 17:30; Matthew 21:28-32; Acts 2:38; 3:19; 5:31; 20:21; 2 Peter 3:9; 2 Corinthians 7:10). And repentance requires undoing the harm done by the wrong acts (Ezekiel 33:14,15; Leviticus 6:1-5; Matthew 21:28-31; Luke 19:8; Philemon 10-14,18,19).

This might involve returning property that we took that belongs to someone else. The thief may have the property in his possession, but it still belongs to the one he stole it from. To truly repent, he must attempt to return it to the rightful owner (compare Ezekiel 33:15). A penitent runaway slave must return to its rightful owner (book of Philemon 10-19). (Compare Acts 26:20; Exodus 22:1-15; Acts 19:18f; Matthew 14:3,4; 1 Corinthians 6:9-11.)

Application to adulterous remarriages

Specifically, when the sin was taking wives from foreign nations, who would influence the Jews to sin, then the only solution would be to get rid of those wives. Similarly, if a man or woman under the gospel has unscripturally divorced and then married someone else, they too are living in a sinful relationship. The marriage was sinful, not just to enter, but also to continue, because it is adultery (Matthew 19:3-9; 5:31,23; Romans. 7:2,3; 1 Corinthians 7:10f). Once again, the only solution would be to cease the marriage relation, just like this case in Ezra's day. A definite agreement and commitment needs to be made in which the couple agrees to separate. Then they must follow through and no longer live together as man and wife.

People want us to think that this is too hard a measure to apply; surely God would not require such sacrifices. Yet He did in this case in Ezra. The people had to give up even their families to make restitution. Jesus plainly said that there would be people who would have to forsake family to serve Him (Luke 14:26; 18:28-30). He said that those who are not willing to do this are not worthy of Him. Yet when it comes down to actual cases, people want to say that surely God would not require such a hard thing!

For further information, see our articles about divorce and remarriage at our Bible Instruction web site at **www.gospelway.com/instruct/**.

Strong spiritual leadership is needed.

Ezra was encouraged to take the leadership and get the job done (verse 4). This would take courage to do, and he was urged to have this courage (compare Josh. 1:5-9). The people in sin need great courage and commitment to make correction, but the leaders of God's people also need great courage and conviction to teach and lead God's people to see the need for such action and to follow through with it.

Such steps are never easy for God's people. The needed change will be made only when the leaders are willing to take a firm Scriptural lead and when the people are willing to follow and make the necessary sacrifices.

10:5-8 – The plan of correction was put into action, and those who would not cooperate would be punished.

Ezra followed through on this plan of action, and required all the guilty people to assemble and put away their wives. He made them take an oath – make the solemn promise required by the covenant that had been agreed upon. This included the leaders and all the people.

He then went into the chamber of Jehohanan, son of Eliashib and there he fasted (eating no bread and drinking no water) and mourned for the guilt of the people. I have no idea who this man was, so apparently it does not matter, except that it was an appropriate place for Ezra to do what needed done. What he did was fast (compare 8:21) and mourn for the sins of the people. This shows again that the sin was terrible, and it illustrates the purpose of fasting as an expression of grief and/or of repentance or special request of God.

The penalty of those who refused to make correction

They issued a proclamation that all the people were to come to Jerusalem to make the arrangements for the guilty men to put away their wives as had been agreed upon (verse 5). The leaders gave the people three days to come. If any would not do so, they would lose their property and would be separated from the people (i.e., the people would "withdraw" from him).

Note that the penalty for refusing to make correction was severe. The sin was great, the correction would be painful, but there were severe penalties for refusing. Likewise, today there must be discipline from the church for members who refuse to correct unscriptural marriages.

In the case of Israel in Ezra's day, the penalty was loss of property and separation from the people. Today, of course, the New Testament nowhere authorizes seizure of property, but it does teach withdrawing from those who practice sin, including fornication. Living in an unscriptural marriage is adultery (a form of fornication). Therefore, as in this case in Ezra, we must withdraw from those who do such and will not make correction. (1 Corinthians 5; 2 Thessalonians 3:6,14,15; Matthew 18:15-17; Titus 3:10,11; Romans 16:17,18; 1 Timothy 1:3-11,19,20; 2 Corinthians 2:6-11)

When we take such measures in these cases today, some people think we are cruel and lack compassion. They claim that such measures go beyond what the Scriptures require. However, God required it in Israel's case here, and the New Testament passages clearly teach it today.

10:9-15 – The people met to make the correction but did it gradually because of the weather and the many people who needed to make correction.

As the leaders had determined, the people gathered in the open square by the temple within the required three days. This occurred on the 20th day of the ninth month of the year (Ezra had just arrived in the fifth month – 7:8,9). But it was a time of heavy rain, so the people trembled because of the serious problem they faced and because of the rain.

Ezra stood before them and taught them of their guilt in taking foreign wives, as has been discussed (compare 9:2). He demanded that they make confession and agree to separate from the people of the land and from the pagan wives.

Confession required

The correction required separation from the foreign wives. But they also had to confess the sin to God. This was required for Israelites who sinned under the law. See Leviticus 26:40-42; Joshua 7:19-21; Proverbs 28:13.

Confession of sin is also required as a condition of forgiveness for children of God today who sin. We must not only repent of the sin, we must pray to God for forgiveness. Then we must change our lives and make restitution. See Acts 8:22; Matthew 6:12; 21:28-32; 1 John 1:8-10.

The congregation's commitment to do right

The congregation responded to Ezra by agreeing they would do as he had taught. However, they appealed to Ezra to give them more time. There were many people involved, it would be a very difficult thing to do, and it was a time of heavy rain.

So they requested that the leaders of the congregation supervise the matter, and let people who were involved in the sin come with their city leaders, each city at an appointed time, till the matter was resolved. In this way they would turn away God's wrath. Note that God's wrath continues until correction is made.

Opposition from within the congregation

Though the people did agree to make correction, there was some opposition. Two men named Jonathan and Jahaziah led the opposition, supported by Meshullam and Shabbethai.

As it was then, so it is today. Sometimes there are those from among God's people who will oppose the efforts of faithful men of God to lead the people to make needed reforms to please God. Change for the good may come only against the will of some within the congregation who ought to support the truth. In particular, sometimes members will say that people in adulterous remarriages do not need to leave their marriages. In such cases, as with Ezra, God's faithful servants must continue on to stand for truth and lead people to obey.

10:16-19 – *The people began ending the sinful marriages.*

As the agreement had been made, the process was begun whereby the people would put away their foreign wives. Ezra and other leaders were in charge of investigating and questioning each man regarding his guilt. From the tenth month to the first month the work continued. So the whole process took a total of three months to complete!

The first ones mentioned as being guilty were actually sons of the priests, even sons of Jeshua the high priest and his brothers! (See regarding Jeshua on 5:2; Haggai 1:1,12.) So indeed the problem did reach to families of some of the very most influential leaders among the people (see 9:2).

All these promised to put away their foreign wives. Then they had to offer the sacrifice for trespass as required by the law. So today, Christians who sin must meet the New Testament conditions of forgiveness (repentance, confession, and prayer); then they must follow through and separate from sinful conduct and relationships.

10:20-44 – *A list of the names of other guilty individuals*

Here is a list of the names of the individuals involved. We may wonder why God would bother to list the names. But there are lessons we can learn.

First, we can learn that the Bible does not hesitate to identify sinners by name. Some today would claim that we should not name people who are guilty of sin, but the Bible does not hesitate to do so. Fortunately, these apparently repented and changed.

Furthermore, such lists help us appreciate that the people who committed this sin and had to leave their wives were real people. These people would have been known to their friends and neighbors. The application of God's law then, like now, was not just a matter of theory. It had practical consequences in personal lives.

Often today, God's people will preach His word about some issue until it affects someone they personally know – perhaps some close friend or family member. Then suddenly they may change their doctrine rather than acknowledge that their loved ones are in sin and must make the necessary sacrifice to correct their lives. This list of names shows us that real people committed real sins and had to make the sacrifice necessary to repent. We must not hesitate today to stand for truth no matter whom we know that is affected by the teaching.

Note the involvement of children in these families.

We are expressly told that some of the wives, that were put away, also had children. This would make it especially hard for the husbands to put them away. Nevertheless, the people obeyed.

Today, the existence of children is often used as an excuse why people in unscriptural marriages must not be required to put away their spouses. Such circumstances are indeed difficult. Not only must the husband and wife give up their marriage, but the children are left without a normal family relationship. But God used this case in Ezra to make it clear that this problem does not justify continuing to live in sin.

10:3 shows that the men not only put away the wives, but also put away the children of those wives. The only reason I can think of for that would relate to the reason why the marriages where sinful to begin with: the pagan wives would influence the people of Israel into sin. Often such influence comes through the children. The children may be influenced into sin by the pagan parent, then the children in turn influence the faithful parent or the children of other families into sin. So the only solution, given the reason why the marriages would be sinful, would be to separate the wives and their children from the congregation. (I see no parallel here to the children of parents today who are in an unscriptural remarriage. This has nothing to do with any guilt or probable guilt of the children. So faithful parents should continue their relationship with their children.)

Conclusion of the book

Under Ezra's guidance, not only had another group of exiled Jews returned to Palestine, but a great spiritual reform had occurred. God's people had been in great error and apostasy. Reform occurred only by diligent effort in the face of great hardship and opposition. This was not easy, but required great sacrifice and commitment. Likewise, it is not easy to reform God's people today either, but we must have the commitment necessary to stand for truth and make the sacrifices needed.

Introduction to the Book of Nehemiah

Background of the Book

Theme

Ezra and Nehemiah give the historical accounts of the return of the Jews from Babylonian captivity. Nehemiah describes the return of the third group from captivity and the rebuilding of the wall of Jerusalem.

Period of Bible History

Restoration from captivity (check our web site to see a timeline of Bible periods: www.gospelway.com/commentary/bible_timeline.pdf).

Author

Some have claimed that the inspired writer of the book was Ezra, but Horne states:

> That Nehemiah, whose name this book bears, and who was cup bearer to Artaxerxes ..., was the author of it, there cannot be any reasonable doubt: the whole of it being written in his name, and, what is very unusual when compared with the preceding sacred historians, being written in the first person.

Summary of book by sections:

Chapter 1-7 – Rebuilding the walls of Jerusalem
Chapter 8-13 – Spiritual restoration of the people

Contemporary prophets

Malachi

Historical Setting

Events in Ezra and Nehemiah occurred during the period of the Jews' return from Babylonian captivity. When the Babylonians had captured Jerusalem and overthrown the nation of Judah, they took the Jews into captivity away from Palestine into Babylon (see 2 Chronicles

36:11-21). But the Medes and Persians later overthrew the Babylonians and began a policy of allowing the Jews to return to Palestine.

There were actually three groups that returned. The first group returned in 536 BC under leadership of Zerubbabel, the second group in 458 BC led by Ezra, and the third group in 445 BC led by Nehemiah.

Consider the history of the period according to the reigns of several great Persian kings (see Chart):

Cyrus — He overthrew Babylon in 538 BC. The first group of Jews returned to Palestine under Zerubbabel's leadership in 536 BC.

Darius the "Great" — During his lifetime, the temple in Jerusalem was rebuilt.

Xerxes — This is the Ahasuerus of the book of Esther. He eventually chose Esther as his queen, and by her influence he saved the Jews from destruction.

Artaxerxes — This man was son of Xerxes and stepson of Esther. He ruled from about 465-423 BC. The books of Ezra and Nehemiah were written during his reign.

Ezra's record begins with the first group that returned under Cyrus. But Ezra himself became personally involved in the story during the 7th year of the reign of Artaxerxes, when Ezra led a group of Jews back to Palestine (458 BC). In the 21st year of the reign, Nehemiah led another group of Jews to return, and rebuilt the walls of Jerusalem.

Practical Lessons

In many ways, the time of Ezra and Nehemiah was like our own. God's people had been in apostasy, which led to the Babylonian captivity. Some leaders had begun the work of restoring the people to God's service, but there were still many problems and the people continued to fall into sin. The task of Ezra and Nehemiah was to provide leadership to continue the restoration and to challenge the people to spiritual faithfulness.

Similarly under the New Testament, after the first century, God's church went into apostasy resulting in the Catholic and Protestant churches. In our age, God's people have sought to return to God and to restore the church. But there are still many problems, and God's people often continue to fall into sin. Strong and faithful leaders are needed to continue the restoration and to challenge God's people to spiritual faithfulness.

We can learn many practical lessons from the problems Ezra and Nehemiah faced and how they dealt with them by God's help.

Review Notes on Nehemiah

As you study the book of Nehemiah, be sure to understand and remember all the material listed below.

1. *Know the 15 periods of Bible history, and the events that mark the beginning and end of each period. Know in which period Nehemiah lived. (See the chart at www.gospelway.com/commentary/bible_timeline.pdf).*

2. *Know the theme of Nehemiah. Know his occupation.*

3. *Steps to useful service to God, as shown by Nehemiah's example:*

a. Care & desire to see God's work prosper.
b. Ask God's help in prayer and be sure your intentions are pleasing to Him.
c. Respect properly ordained authority.
d. Determine what action is needed, and develop a plan of action.
e. Motivate people to work.
f. Resist opposition.
g. Rebuke sin among God's people.
h. Be willing to make personal sacrifices and set a good example.
i. Teach God's word and encourage people to worship Him.
j. Lead people to recognize their sin and repent of it.
k. Lead people to commit themselves to obey God's will.
l. Remind people of their commitment to God, and rebuke disobedience.

4. *Methods of opposition to God's work, and how to deal with them, as shown by Nehemiah's example*

(Note: be able to name the 3 men that led the opposition against Nehemiah):

a. Mockery & discouragement — Handle this by appealing to God, trusting and praying to Him; rebuke the opponents; keep working.
b. Threats of warfare/attacks — Handle this by appealing to God, organizing people to fight evil, always be on guard, and keep working.
c. Offers to meet and compromise — Handle this by refusing to compromise or to meet if it hinders the work; keep working.
d. Accusations of self-serving motives — Handle this by denying the accusations, point out the lack of proof, appeal to God, and keep working.
e. Attempts to cause fear or encourage sin that will discredit workers — Handle this by refusing to violate God's word, consider the influence of your conduct, trust God, and keep working.

f. Attempts to weaken opposition to error by means of compromising people — Handle this by keeping working.

5. How to deal with sin among God's people, as shown by Nehemiah's example:

a. Be concerned enough to see the need for change.
b. Think carefully and determine a Scriptural plan of action.
c. Confront people who sinned and call on them to repent.
d. Discuss the error before an assembly of God's people.
e. Present the evidence on which you base your conclusions.
f. Offer a Scriptural solution.
g. Expect people to repent, make restitution, and bring forth fruits of repentance.
h. Reach a definite plan of reconciliation, and expect all parties to do as promised.

6. The cycle of Israel's relationship to God, as described in Neh. 9, can be illustrated as follows:

Sin then Deliverance then Defeat then Repentance (repeat)

7. The following steps are illustrated in Neh. 8-13 as necessary steps in spiritual conversion and restoration:

a. Study and learn God's law (chapter 8). (Note the methods used to study God's law. Also remember the people's attitude in learning. Note that the people were able to understand God's will and restore their relationship to God by following a message written hundreds of years earlier.)
b. Recognize and confess God's goodness and man's sinfulness (chapter 9).
c. Make a commitment to obey God's word (chapter 10).
d. Follow through and practice the obedience that was committed (chapter 13).

8. Neh. 13 lists 4 specific ways that the Jews had violated their covenant to serve God, and/or had disobeyed God's law:

a. Tobiah's personal possessions were kept in the temple chamber.
b. The Levites' provisions had not been given to them.
c. People were working and doing business on the Sabbath.
d. People were inter-marrying with those who were not God's people.

Part 1: Rebuilding of the Walls of Jerusalem - Chapter 1-7

Nehemiah Chapter 1

Nehemiah Learns the Conditions in Jerusalem - Chapter 1

1:1 – Introduction to the man Nehemiah in Shushan, the palace of the king of Persia

The book is introduced as the words of Nehemiah, son of Hachaliah. This could mean, either that he wrote the book, or that the story records his life and words but someone else actually recorded it. Many people believe Ezra wrote the book, because it is so similar to his writings. But it is spoken in the first person as though Nehemiah himself is speaking.

Little is known of Nehemiah except what is written in this book. He was apparently recognized as an important person in many ways. He had the serious responsibility of being the king's cupbearer (see on v11). The Persian king readily named him governor of Judea (10:1). So, like Daniel and Esther, he was a Jew who became prominent in the nation of his captivity. Nothing is known for sure about his father Hachaliah.

The story begins in the month Chislev in the 20th year. 2:1 shows this means the 20th year of the reign of Persian king Artaxerxes (see chart). The Waldrons state that Artaxerxes started to reign in 465BC, so these events would have taken place beginning in 445 BC.

Artaxerxes had been king when Ezra brought his group of exiles back to Judah in the 7th year of the king (Ezra 7:1,8). So it was 13 years from the time Ezra brought his group to Judah till the time Nehemiah's story began.

Nehemiah served in Shushan, the palace of the king of Persia. This was the same place where Esther earlier had lived and served as queen in the book of Esther (Esther 1:2). Remember that events in the book of Nehemiah actually occurred after the events in the book of Esther (see introduction).

Step #1 to Useful Service to God: Really Care and Desire To See God's Work and God's People Prosper.

1:2,3 – Nehemiah's brother reported that the wall of the city of Jerusalem was still broken down.

Nehemiah received a visit from Hanani who is identified as one of his brothers (compare 7:2) who came with other men from Judah. At this time two groups of Jews had returned to Judah from captivity (see introduction). Apparently some of these came back for a visit to their relatives in Shushan.

Nehemiah asked these men about the welfare of the Jews who had returned from captivity to Jerusalem. This question led to a discussion that informed Nehemiah about the problems in Judah, which in turn introduces the theme of the book.

The visitors informed Nehemiah that the remnant of the people in Jerusalem were facing severe problems. They were in distress and reproach. The city wall was broken down and the gates burned with fire. The Babylonians had done this when they overthrew the city (2 Kings 25:8-10; 2 Chronicles 36:19; Jeremiah 52:12-14). There is no record that repairs had been made to the wall by the first two groups that had returned. If they had attempted repairs, they did not complete the work and whatever work they had done had fallen into disrepair again. Remember, it had been ninety years since the first group had returned.

The subsequent story will help us understand the significance of this problem. But cities in those days needed walls for protection from enemies. Also a destroyed wall symbolized a city in defeat and desolation (compare 2:17).

We will see that these problems deeply grieved Nehemiah. This was a time of restoration and rebuilding the nation that had fallen because of apostasy. The Jews had returned to rebuild the city and restore the nation. But Nehemiah was grieved by the evidence that they were so far from achieving that goal.

God's people in our own day also face serious needs.

The problems the Jews faced in Nehemiah's day had begun because of their apostasy from God's way. Some restoration had occurred, but there were still problems and challenges. Likewise, many problems have occurred because people have departed from God's plan for the New Testament.

Much has been done to restore the service of God among His true people, though many who claim to serve Him yet remain in apostasy. But even among those who have come so far in the restoration, there remain many problems to be dealt with: worldliness, neglect of God's work, divorce and remarriage, perversion of church organization and work, sexual laxity (immodesty, dancing), immoral entertainment, humanism, family problems, lack of dedicated leaders, profanity, smoking, drinking, lack of Bible study and prayer, and negligence in spreading the gospel.

Some congregations of God's people are doing fairly well in these areas, but in many congregations the wall is broken down and the gates have been burned. What is our reaction? Consider Nehemiah's reaction when he learned of the problems in Judah.

1:4 – Nehemiah wept and fast in response to the news.

When Nehemiah heard the condition of God's people, he wept and mourned, fasted, and prayed to God. This continued for "many days," not just a few minutes. Note that fasting was an expression of his sorrow and grief, associated with prayer to God (compare on Ezra 8:21; 9:3ff; 10:1ff).

We too should be concerned and troubled when we see God's people are in trouble. We should not just overlook it or shake our heads and go about our business. We should be truly sad to know the problems and weaknesses that exist in the lives of members. We should go to God in prayer for His help. And we should grieve to the point of seeking to work to overcome the problems.

How much does it bother you to see problems and spiritual failings in the lives of God's people?

Step #2 In Useful Service to God: Seek God's Help in Prayer and Be Sure Our Intentions Please Him.

1:5 – Nehemiah began praising God's faithfulness.

The following verses summarize Nehemiah' prayer after he heard of the distress of the Jews in Jerusalem. The record gives a good lesson on the content of prayer.

Nehemiah honored God as the God of heaven, the great and awesome God. He keeps His covenant and shows mercy to those who love Him and keep His commands.

The God of the Bible is the one true God, ruler of heaven and earth. He deserves our worship and praise. He keeps His word and respects His promises. When He agrees to do a thing, we can trust Him to do it. When covenants are broken, we can be sure that it is man who has broken them, not God.

God has mercy and loving kindness toward men. He cares what happens to us. But we benefit from His love conditionally: we must love Him and keep His commands. Such a God gives us a reason to pray and hope that He will answer.

Our prayers should not just make requests for things we want for ourselves. We should also express praise for God's greatness. This praise was especially appropriate because Nehemiah was about to ask God to do the thing he just praised God for: to keep His covenant and show mercy on His people.

1:6,7 – *He confessed the sins and disobedience of the people.*

Having praised God, Nehemiah then begged Him to open His eyes, be attentive, and hear the prayer Nehemiah was about to offer. He said he was in prayer day and night about this matter. Note the frequency and duration of prayer: night and day over a period of many days – verse 4 (not just a few hours a week whenever the church is meeting).

Nehemiah prayed on behalf of God's servants, the children of Israel, not just for something he wanted for himself. He prayed for others, the whole nation in this case.

He then confessed and acknowledged the sins of the people. Israel had sinned; Nehemiah and his family had sinned. He openly admits their corrupt conduct toward God, that they had not kept God's commands, statutes, and ordinances given through Moses. Compare Ezra 10:1; Nehemiah 9:2; Daniel 9:20.

Today we are obligated to keep, not Moses' law, but Jesus' law in the gospel. Nevertheless, we must confess when we sin under the gospel (see Matthew 6:12; Luke 18:9-14; Acts 8:22; 1 John 1:9).

1:8,9 – *He recalled God's promises to return the people from captivity.*

Nehemiah then reminded God of His promises to Israel. Through Moses God had commanded Israel that He would scatter them among the nations if they were unfaithful. But if they would then repent and keep His commands, He would gather them and bring them back to the land chosen as His dwelling place – no matter where they were scattered, He could and would do this. Moses wrote this in Leviticus 26:14,15,33,39; Deuteronomy 4:25-31; 28:15,36,63-67; 30:1-10.

God had truly kept His word in this. The people had been unfaithful and He surely had scattered them across the world for those sins. Now Nehemiah was urging God to keep the second part of the promise: to return the people when they repented and bless them again in the land.

Likewise, God has made plain promises to us under the gospel, and we have every right to claim those promises in prayer. He has promised forgiveness of sins, the hope of eternal life, strength to overcome temptation, blessings in raising our families, etc. We have every right to believe God will keep His promises in these matters if we live to serve Him.

1:10,11 – *He sought God's help in his request of the king.*

Nehemiah then reminded God that he was making request on behalf of God's own servants, the people He had redeemed by His mighty power. He was not making request on his own behalf. Here is another lesson for us: we surely may pray for things we ourselves need, but we should also remember to pray for the needs of others, especially God's people.

Nehemiah again called on God to hear his prayer and the prayer of others who feared Him. He then came to the specific point of his prayer. He wanted God to bless and prosper him in his effort to make request of the king. At this point we are not told exactly what request he wanted to make; however, the next chapter immediately reveals that Nehemiah wanted the king to empower him to go back to help the Jews with the problems Nehemiah had heard about. We are not even told exactly what "man" it was that he wanted mercy in his eyes. However, this is clearly hinted at by telling us Nehemiah was cupbearer to the king.

Note that we likewise need to pray to God for the things that are truly important in life, especially for His blessings on our work for Him. We should realize that our strength and success comes from Him, and we will prosper only if we have His blessings. Without Him we can do nothing. When we see problems in our families or in the church, we should be willing to work to meet the need. But we must also seek God's blessings in prayer.

Nehemiah's occupation: cupbearer to the king

Finally, the chapter tells us Nehemiah's occupation: he was the cupbearer to the king. This was not a trivial job: carrying around a cup. It was a serious responsibility, like current security police who work to protect the president. The cupbearer's job was to make sure that no one poisoned the king. He was to constantly supervise all that the king drank to be sure no harm came to him.

As cupbearer, Nehemiah was a very trusted servant. He would also be a constant companion to the king, present or at least nearby every time the king drank anything (compare chapter 2). The effect would be to even give him access to the king as a friend or possibly even a counselor.

Nehemiah Chapter 2

Nehemiah Returns and Organizes the Work – Chapter 2,3

Step #3 in Useful Service to God: Where Possible, Obtain Permission and Assistance from People in Authority

2:1-3 – When the king asked about Nehemiah's sadness, he explained conditions in the city of Jerusalem.

The king asked the reasons for Nehemiah sadness.

The events recorded here occurred in the month Nisan in the twentieth year of Artaxerxes. Nehemiah was serving wine to the king, as his work required (1:11). Note that "wine" in the Bible does not always mean fermented or intoxicating wine, as the term generally implies today. See Isaiah 16:10; 65:8; Jeremiah 48:33; Genesis 40:9-11; Revelation 19:15.

Nehemiah had not in the past been sad or sorrowful in disposition, when he was in the presence of the king. However, on this occasion he appeared to be sad, and the king noticed it and asked the cause. He knew Nehemiah was not physically ill, so he concluded it was sorrow of heart. He was upset in mind. See Proverbs 15:13.

This gave Nehemiah the opportunity he had been praying for to ask the king's help (1:11). But when the time came, Nehemiah was beset by great fear. Note that serving God is not always easy or without emotional hardship. The record helps us see Nehemiah's emotions. First, he had great sorrow when he heard of the troubles in Jerusalem. Now he had great fear before the king. Those who please God are not those who manage to avoid facing emotional fears and griefs, but those who conquer them to do God's will despite the hardships.

The account does not directly state why Nehemiah was fearful, but if we would put ourselves in his place we can see several reasons why we might be fearful. He was about to make a great request of the greatest ruler on the face of the earth. One would not lightly enter such a request. There was the possibility that the king could become so angry he could punish Nehemiah. Or at the least he could deny the request and demand that Nehemiah stay in Shushan and not leave. In any case, the possibilities were so important to Nehemiah that he feared for the result. Waldron also says that it was improper for servants of the king to allow their personal lives to affect their service and demeanor before the king, but Nehemiah's sorrow had become obvious.

Nehemiah told the king about his concerns for Jerusalem.

Nehemiah responded first by expressing great respect for the king. He said, "Let the king live forever!" This is similar to the modern expression, "Long live the king!" This was a common expression for praising the king. It showed people valued the king and wanted his service as king to continue (though of course no one physically lives forever in the absolute sense). See 1 Kings 1:31; Daniel 2:4; 5:10; 6:6,21. Wisdom would teach us to speak respectfully to people in positions of power, especially when we have a great request to make of them.

Nehemiah then explained that it was only reasonable for him to be troubled considering the problems in his homeland. The city where his fathers had lived and been buried now lay in waste and its gates consumed by fire (see notes on 1:3,4). This was Nehemiah's concern, so he used the opportunity to honestly speak to the king about it.

2:4-8 – *Nehemiah asked permission to return and rebuild the wall, and that the king would help make provisions.*

The king was clearly a perceptive, wise king. He knew Nehemiah sought the king's help regarding this matter, so he asked what Nehemiah wanted.

Before answering, Nehemiah offered another prayer to God. Note the importance of prayer in Nehemiah's service to God. He had already prayed many days about this (see 1:4ff). Now he had a receptive response from the king, but he knew he needed greater help than that of the king. So he went to God in prayer. It could not have been a long prayer, and probably was not spoken out loud, since he was in the king's presence and had to give an answer. Yet his prayer shows the need for seeking God's help, especially in important works we seek to do for Him. We should imitate such examples. (1 John 5:14,15; 3:21,22; James 5:16; Matthew 7:7-11; 18:19; 1 Peter 5:7; John 14:13,14; compare 1 Samuel 1:10-28; 7:5-11; 2 Kings 20:1-7; 2 Chronicles 7:11-14).

Nehemiah made several requests:

(1) First, he asked the king for permission to go to Jerusalem to rebuild the city. This request, of course, was his response to the information he had received in chapter 1 about the serious problems the city faced. We are told that the queen was also present on this occasion.

The king, as would be appropriate before making such a decision, asked for specifics. He wanted to know how long the trip would take and when Nehemiah would return. Note that he assumed Nehemiah would want to return.

We are then expressly told that the king was favorable to Nehemiah's request and granted it. Nehemiah set a time (apparently for when he would leave). He had evidently thought this out well ahead of time, and he had a specific plan to propose.

Nehemiah's plan, however, involved yet more requests of the king.

(2) Next he asked for letters to the governors in the territory that he would pass through, giving him authority to travel to Judah. Since the entire area was subject to the king of Persia, the local governors would be required to cooperate with Nehemiah and not cause him trouble, if he had letters of authority from the king. ("Beyond the river" probably refers to the territories on the other side of the Euphrates – see NKJV footnote.)

(3) Nehemiah's third request was for a letter to a man named Asaph, who supervised the forests of the king. Nehemiah wanted this man to be required to provide the timber that would be needed to rebuild the city gates and wall of Jerusalem and a house for Nehemiah himself. We will see that the house was not just for Nehemiah's benefit, but he was very generous in caring for others (see on chapter 5).

The king was favorable and granted all Nehemiah's requests. But Nehemiah gave thanks to God for this favorable result. He had repeatedly made request of God for these blessings, so it was only right that he then give God credit when the blessings were granted. We should remember this too in our prayers to God.

Step #4 in Useful Service: Develop a Plan of Action

2:9,10 – Nehemiah returned to Judah, but people of the land opposed his plans.

Nehemiah says nothing about the journey from Persia to Judah. However, the third group of Jews at this point returned to Judah under the leadership of Nehemiah.

He immediately proceeded to discuss the activities after his return. He first delivered to the governors of the region the letters that the king had given him. This would show them the authority for his work.

In addition, though the record does not mention Nehemiah's request for such help, the king had sent captains and horsemen in the army with him.

As in the book of Ezra, when God's people begin to work effectively for Him, you can be sure there will be opposition. These verses introduce the villains of the story. They are Sanballat the Horonite and Tobiah the Ammonite. Later accounts include Geshem the Arabian (see 2:19; 4:1). These men were greatly upset that someone had come to help the Israelites with their problems.

We may wonder why anyone would oppose efforts to help the Jews. The answer, of course, is that these men were all enemies of the Jews. Nehemiah 4:2 tells us that Sanballat was with the army of Samaria. This meant he was part of the mixed breed of Samaritans who had been brought into the land by the Assyrians after they removed the northern tribes of Israel into captivity. As such, they were not real Israelites and had no inheritance in Israel (2:20). Their worship to God was a perversion, which professed to serve God but included idol worship. See notes on Ezra 4:1-3 to see how the first group of returning exiles had forbidden these false worshipers to participate with them in building the temple.

Tobiah was an Ammonite. The Ammonites were descendants of Abraham's nephew Lot. They lived near the desert east of the Jordan River. Geshem was an Arab. The Arabians have not been mentioned much in the Old Testament and appear to have traveled from place to place without settling in any one area. By this time, however, at least some of these people must have lived in or near the area of Jerusalem. So they were not happy to see the Jews prosper.

All three of these men apparently had some local authority. The fact they are mentioned immediately after Nehemiah reported to the governors may imply they were among the governors. Otherwise, they soon heard the news from Nehemiah's meeting with the governors. We will see the problems they caused as the story progressed and how Nehemiah and the Jews dealt with them.

2:11,12 – *Nehemiah observed the condition of the wall.*

Having arrived in Jerusalem, Nehemiah waited three days. Then he went out at night to view the wall. He took a few men with him, but he had not yet told anyone of his intentions. He did not even take an animal except the one he rode on.

A principle of good leadership is that, before one begins he must develop a plan. He must know exactly what work needs to be done. What needs exist, and what problems can be expected? Then one must determine where to start and how to proceed.

Too often people jump into a project without having thought it through. They are disorganized, have no plan, and have set no priorities. This often leads to discouragement and failure. Nehemiah began by inspecting the situation so he could formulate a plan.

2:13-15 – A summary of the areas Nehemiah viewed

He went out by night through the Valley Gate then to the Serpent Well (Jackal's Well – ASV). Then he went to the Refuse or Dung Gate. From there he went to the Fountain Gate then to the King's pool. Exactly where all these points were in the wall, I do not know.

But as he went, he viewed the condition of the wall and the gates. We are told little except that, at the King's pool there was no room for the animal to pass. Presumably this is told to indicate that the rubble was so bad it was impassable for his animal.

Then he returned to the Valley Gate by which he had begun.

Step #5 in Useful Service: Motivate People to Work

2:16-18 – When Nehemiah described the problem to the Jewish leaders, they decided to rise and build.

The other officials of the Jews knew nothing about Nehemiah's plan. He had told them nothing of his purpose nor of his investigation of the wall. At this point, however, he met with them and explained to them his plan.

First, he challenged them by describing the problem they faced. He talked about the distress they faced because the city was still laid waste (specifically referring to the wall), and the gates had been burned (see on 1:3). The people, of course, knew this. But sometimes people live with a situation so long they fail to see the seriousness of the problem. They had done little or nothing about it for years, so Nehemiah had to begin by motivating them to see how bad things were so they would want to do something about it.

He urged them to build the wall so they would no longer be a reproach. The wall was a source of protection, but to be without the wall was also a reminder to them and everyone else that they were a defeated, fallen, and defenseless nation. The city had been destroyed because of their sin. To restore the wall would indicate a restoration of their favor with God and of their commitment as a nation to work for Him.

Likewise, Jesus' church often faces difficult situations. Sometimes we have internal problems. Sometimes we are just few in number or have few members that are mature and committed. Sometimes we face doctrinal strife, immorality among the members, or just general ignorance and indifference. Sometimes the problem is just that there are so many lost souls around us in need of hearing the truth. In any case, the members need to be motivated to work, and one way to do so is to describe to them honestly the problems they face.

He told them of the advantages they had and urged them to work.

He then told the people of the good that had already been accomplished. God had blessed Nehemiah so the king had given permission for the work. Note that Nehemiah continues to give God the credit. In order for the work to prosper, the people needed the provisions the king offered as well as the authority to do the work. Nehemiah had already obtained this.

Note that Nehemiah motivated the people by telling the good as well as the bad. He told of the work that needed to be done, but he also gave them reason to believe they could do it. We need to do the same in motivating ourselves to work for God. Yes, we often face great problems. But let us not be discouraged but trust in God to provide what we need to accomplish His work. He can give the victory if we will use what He provides.

The people responded with a will to work.

They said, "Let us rise up and build!" They then strengthened their hands for the work. That is, they made the necessary preparations. They did not just talk about it, but they immediately proceeded to do what was needed to accomplish the job. This is exactly the attitude that God's people need today.

Note that sometimes people are able to do a work for the Lord and would be willing to do so, if they simply have good leadership to challenge them. This job had been waiting for years to be done. When the challenge was presented, they responded. What was lacking was dedicated leadership. We should also remember this need today.

Step #6 in Useful Service: Resist Opposition

2:19,20 – The first attempt at opposition: ridicule and mockery was answered by faith in God.

Sanballat, Tobiah, and Geshem had been unfavorable to the Jew's project since they first heard of it (verse 10). These verses reveal the beginning of their active efforts to frustrate the work.

The opposition

As with most enemies, their first attempt was to discourage the work by speaking against it. They laughed at the people and expressed their hatred and spite. Then they implied that the action constituted rebellion against the king. This would have been a serious charge, if true. We remember that such a charge had caused a halt in the work on the temple in Ezra 4.

Likewise today, when we attempt to seriously restore the Lord's church according to His standard, people often ridicule us and tell us we cannot possibly succeed. They express hatred, hoping that simply their expressions of disapproval will discourage us to the point we give up the attempt. They call us Campbellites, antis, Bible-beaters, orphan-haters, etc. They accuse us of believing in water salvation, salvation by works, not following the spirit of Jesus, judging others, etc.

Note that these statements, both in Nehemiah's case and in our case today, are made without proof. Often no attempt is made whatever to prove them. There was no evidence the people were rebelling against the king. On the contrary, they had express authority from the king to do exactly as they were doing. Likewise, we have Bible authority for our teaching and practice. But people hope that just the accusations will be enough to discourage God's people till we quit. Or at least they hope to discredit us and prejudice others against us, so they will not join with us but will join the opposition against us. People do not like to be ridiculed, and often such tactics lead at least some people to refuse to work for God.

See Matthew 5:10-12; 13:21; 27:27-31,39-44; Luke 6:22,23; John 15:20; 16:33; Acts 14:22; Romans 5:3; 8:17-39; 2 Corinthians 1:4-10; 4:17; 7:4; 2 Timothy 3:12; Hebrews 10:32-36; 1 Peter 2:19-23; 3:14-18; 4:1,15-19; 5:10

Nehemiah's response to the ridicule

Such ridicule and spite needs to be answered, at least at first (compare chapter 6) and at least to the people of God, so they will not be discouraged by it.

Nehemiah responded that God would prosper the Jews in their work, so they would proceed with the work trusting in Him. People may ridicule and say it cannot be done, but if we are on God's side, He will provide what we need.

Then Nehemiah argued that these enemies had no portion, right, or memorial in Jerusalem. In short, this was not their job. They had no right to be involved in it anyway, so why should the people pay any attention to them? They were not really Jews, but were people of other nations. Their service to God was a perversion, so the Jews would not allow them to participate in the work even if they had wanted to do so. See notes on Ezra 4:3,4 (compare Neh. 4:2). In essence, Nehemiah was saying it was "none of their business."

We must always remember whom we work for, whom we seek to please, and who is the source of our strength. If we work for people or to please people, such as these enemies, then it might make sense to quit if they are displeased by our work. But if they are not the ones we seek to please, if they ultimately have no power over us, and if they are not involved in the work anyway, why should we care what they think or say? Why should their opinions alter our work?

Too often we are unduly influenced by people who have no right to influence us. They will not ultimately be our judges. They will not determine our reward. They cannot ultimately bless or punish us. We are working for Someone far greater and more important, Who can give us a true reward. We must ignore those feeble humans who oppose us and determine instead to please the One who is our Master, Judge, and source of our eternal reward. Acts 5:29; Heb. 13:5,6.

Nehemiah Chapter 3

3:1-32 – The assignments of the workers
This chapter describes the labor of various groups who worked to rebuild the wall. Various people are named and their areas of labor are described. The description begins at the Sheep Gate, then moves section by section around the wall till it returns again to the Sheep Gate (compare verses 1,32).

The only information worth special observation is verse 5, which says that some of the nobles did not put their necks to the work of the Lord. This appears to be a rebuke. Prosperous people often expect other people to work while they do as they please. They seem to think they are above menial labor. But this was a work for all to do, both for their own protection and for the good of the nation. Above all, it was a work God wanted done. We should all learn to work for the Lord without excuses.

Value of this information
One may wonder why these details are recorded in Scripture. Surely such details are not necessary for us to know in order to be saved, so why did God include them? We may not know for sure all the reasons why, but here are some benefits the information has:

1) It demonstrates the ***historical*** nature of the record. Naming specific people and specific places where they worked, especially with such detailed descriptions, serves no purpose whatever unless the account is intended to be taken as history. This confirms that we should view the record as historic fact.

2) It shows that the work was done in an ***organized*** manner. This shows us the value of working for God in an organized way. Everyone should be given work to do, and each one should know what is expected of them.

3) It helps us appreciate the magnitude of the job.

4) It gives recognition and appreciation to the laborers. Each of them is permanently recorded by name in God's word.

There may someday be other value to the record that we cannot now foresee. Perhaps the description will someday be verified by archiaeologists or will serve some other purpose in confirming Scripture.

In any case, God chose to record these people and their work for the sake of future information.

Nehemiah Chapter 4

Enemies Oppose the Work – Chapter 4

First Method of Opposition: Mockery and Discouragement

4:1-3 – The enemies' anger led them to ridicule the work.

The opposition of Sanballat and his companions had begun in chapter 2. When they had heard of the work, they had mocked and ridiculed. In this chapter the opposition continued and significantly intensified. We will see how Nehemiah and the Jews dealt with it. From their example, we can learn important lessons about how we today should deal with the opposition we face in service to God. See notes on Ezra 4.

God's people have always faced opposition in their work for God. People are rarely truly neutral about God and His true work. Either they support and defend it, or they oppose it. The methods of opposition are similar from generation to generation, so we can learn from the examples here.

Sanballat's ridicule

Sanballat had been introduced in 2:10,19. He had been upset to hear that Nehemiah had come to work for the benefit of the Jews. Here he became even angrier as he heard the work on the wall had actually begun and was progressing.

His first effort to prevent the work had been mockery and attempts to discourage the work (2:19). Here he continued those tactics but in more extreme forms. He evidently hoped that he could discourage the Jews from succeeding by mocking their efforts and reminding them of the enormity of the task they faced.

He appeared with his brethren, the army of Samaria. This shows that Sanballat was a Samaritan, part of the people that the Assyrians had moved into the area after they removed the Israelites. Intermarriage with various other people had made them a mixed race. In any case, they had no real inheritance in Israel (see on 2:10).

Sanballat began taunting the Israelites that they were too feeble to do the job they had begun. He points out the greatness of the task. Did they think they were strong enough to build fortifications? Were they able to make sacrifices? Did they think they had begun a job that could be completed easily with little work, like a one-day job? He pointed out the heaps of rubbish that stood in their way, much of which had been burned. Did they think they could raise stone walls from the rubbish? This turned out to be a real concern (see 4:10).

No doubt all these were real problems, and Nehemiah and the Jews had surely considered them. But Sanballat's intent appears to be to discourage the workers by convincing them they could never complete so great a task, so why bother to try?

Tobiah joins the ridicule.

Tobiah then joined the mockery by saying the wall the Jews built was so feeble that it would fall down if a fox or jackal stepped on it. This was obviously an exaggeration, but the purpose was to make the people think their work was not worthwhile. He hoped they would view the effort as not being worth the attempt.

We face similar ridicule today.

People attempt to discourage us saying how small and weak our efforts are. The church is small and many people disagree with us. We are a minority opposing large churches with powerful hierarchies and wealthy organizations. We have no political power, no wealth, no influential members, and no seminary-trained preachers, so how can we succeed?

But remember, if people really thought it was impossible for us to succeed, they would not bother to say anything or do anything at all! People do not bother to oppose what they truly believe to be ineffective. They just laugh and go about their business. The very fact they find us worth their time and effort to refute proves they feel at least somewhat threatened by our work.

4:4-6 – Nehemiah responded with prayer and trust in God, so the wall was built to half its height.

Nehemiah dealt with the discouragement by going to the ultimate source of strength: He appealed to God in prayer. Likewise, when we are taunted regarding our apparent weaknesses, we should remember that true strength is not ultimately found in any of the sources that people say we lack. True strength does not lie in numbers, wealth, influence, etc. True strength lies in God and His word. So when we face discouragement and ridicule, we too need to turn to God and the strength He can supply. (Compare Psalms 123:3,4.)

Nehemiah called on God to hear their taunting and be aware of the fact that His people were despised. He called on God to turn the reproach back on those who spoke the reproach. That is, let the people suffer who wanted to cause suffering to God's people. (Compare Psalms 79:12.) They did the wrong, so let them suffer for it, instead of God's people suffering.

He said God could even send them as captives to a foreign land. This is the punishment that God had put on the Jews for their rebellion against Him. Now they had returned to serving Him and had come back to the land, and now they were being mocked for the weakness that had come upon them. A fitting punishment for those who mocked them would be for them to now be sent into captivity!

Further, he called on God to not cover or overlook the iniquity of the enemies – they had not repented of it, so they should not be allowed to go unpunished but should be punished even as the Jews had when they had refused to repent of their sins. The things the enemies had said were not just a reproach on the people who were building the wall; they were a reproach on God Himself, because it was God's work the people were doing. (Compare Psalms 69:27,28; 109:14,15; Jer. 18:23.)

Likewise, when people today revile the people of God who are doing His work, they are actually reproaching God. Such conduct angers God and is worthy of punishment.

The people then continued the work.

Having prayed for strength, Nehemiah and the people just kept working. The result was that the wall was built and completely joined together to half of its height. Clearly God's blessing was behind this work, but it was also possible because the people had a mind to work.

God does not bless those who will not work for Him. So to be successful, first we must trust in God, then we must be willing to work for Him: Trust and obey, faith and works. If we think we cannot succeed in God's work, and if we look at our own weaknesses and problems, then we get discouraged and do not work. But when we trust God and work willingly, He can accomplish through us much more than we even thought possible.

Are we of a mind to work in the church today? Could it be that the church is often unsuccessful in God's work today, not because we are lacking numbers and wealth, etc., but because we do not trust in God enough to work diligently at the work He has given us? Instead of having a mind to work for God, could it be we have a mind to make money for our own benefit and enjoy pleasure, entertainment, sports, TV, and other activities for ourselves instead of for God?

Second Method of Opposition: Plots of Violence and Warfare

4:7-9 – The enemies conspired to attack and create confusion.

The enemies' opposition

Sanballat and Tobiah, along with their companions the Arabs, Ammonites, and Ashdodites, heard that the work on the wall was progressing and prospering. The walls were being restored and the gaps were being closed. This made the enemies very angry. Enemies of the truth today are likewise especially angry when they see our work for God is progressing and prospering.

So the enemies determined to move on to more extreme measures. They plotted to attack the workers in the city and create confusion. If they attacked while the wall was still incomplete, they might succeed in causing such confusion, disorganization, and discouragement that the work would stop.

This has often been the pattern of the enemies of truth. First they mock and ridicule God's people. But if that does not stop the work, then they move on to physical violence or threats of violence. Many examples exist in the early history of the gospel. Consider the deaths of John (Matt. 14), Jesus (Matt. 27), Stephen (Acts 7), and James (Acts 12). Consider the imprisonment of Peter (Acts 4,5,12) and Paul (Acts 16; etc.), and others (Acts 8).

While our society frowns on physical violence against religious people, it is sometimes threatened. And imprisonment is not unknown. And who knows what the future holds?

Nehemiah responded by further prayer and setting a watch.

The response to the mockery and ridicule had been based on prayer to God. When the opposition became more extreme, more prayer was needed. Some lose faith when the opposition is not easily overcome. They think God does not hear them or does not care. But Nehemiah continued to trust God and just encouraged more prayer.

But again they responded with work as well as prayer. They set a watch against the enemies day and night. That is, they assigned people to be on guard to watch for the enemy to attack. Then the Jews could be warned to defend themselves. Note that we are responsible to work to bring about what we pray for. Prayer is not an excuse to leave everything to God while we do nothing. Rather it obligates us to do what we can.

So today when people plan to do violence to God's people, we need to continue to pray. And it is appropriate for us to be watchful for the harm they can do us. Of course, we do not respond with physical violence – neither Jesus nor His disciples ever defended themselves with force against their spiritual enemies (John 18:36). We fight a spiritual battle (Eph. 6:12), so we must be on guard spiritually for the spiritual attacks of Satan and his people (1 Peter 5:8; 2 Cor. 10:3-5)).

4:10-12 – The people became discouraged and fearful.

At this point the pressures of the task and the threats of the enemies began to take a toll on the people, and they did begin to become discouraged. Some warned Nehemiah that there was so much rubbish that the people could not work on the wall. The strength of the people was failing. They began to think they could not finish the job.

Likewise the enemies continued their pressures. They plotted sneak attacks in which they would come unexpectedly into the midst of the people and kill some of them. They hoped this would cause the work to cease. Apparently they did not realize the Nehemiah was aware of their plans, or perhaps they thought they could still attack unexpectedly and create enough havoc to defeat the work.

Note how similar this is to modern terrorism: unexpected sneak attacks that kill innocent citizens with the hope of discouraging the people till they give in to the terrorists' demands. Such plots are nothing new. We will see how Nehemiah dealt with them.

The knowledge of this danger began to cause the Jews to become fearful, especially those who lived closest to the enemies. Ten times they came to Nehemiah appealing for protection. They implied that the enemies would attack at whatever place Nehemiah turned from – i.e., when he moved away from an area, that is where the attack would come. He could not be everywhere at once and defend everyone, so they were insecure.

Important works face critical times of discouragement.

Such points of discouragement are typical in the course of important tasks. When the work first begins, people are enthusiastic. The enthusiasm carries them over the hurdles and hardships. And when the task nears its end, people can see that the end is at hand, so they are encouraged to continue working to see it through. But somewhere in the middle of the task often comes a point of discouragement in which people are not sure they are able to finish.

Often this is a combination, as in this case, of internal and external problems. People within the group begin to grumble and complain or become discouraged. People outside the group are attempting to make the work as difficult as possible. So the enormity of the task combined with opposition of enemies begins to take its toll.

Nehemiah and the people faced such a critical time, and we often do likewise in our work today. If we can get through these times and still keep on working, often we can get the job done. But if we allow the discouragement to overwhelm us, we fail.

4:13-15 – Nehemiah stationed armed guards and urged the people to trust in God.

Nehemiah was wise enough to realize that the work was at a critical point and that steps could be taken and needed to be taken to keep the work going. First he positioned people with weapons at the openings in the wall and behind the lower parts of the wall. Here he grouped them by families.

This appears to me to be a means of providing protection at the weakest points of the wall, perhaps combined with a measure to make sure all the people were within the safety of the wall. Instead of being exposed in those areas near the enemies (verse 12), the people and their families would be behind the walls. This is expressly stated to be the case at night in verse 22.

Then he gave the leaders and the people encouragement. He reminded them that they did not need to be paralyzed by fear; they should not act as cowards, but be strong. First, he reminded them that God was on their side. He would fight for them, as He had so many times in the past (Num. 14:9; Deut. 1:29; 2 Sam. 10:12). This did not mean they would not have to fight, but it meant that God's strength would sustain them in that fight.

Then he urged them to be willing to fight for their families and property: their wives, sons, daughters, brothers, and homes.

Note that his plan did not include giving in to the threats of the enemies. When we give up the work and give in to the demands of terrorists and those who threaten us, we have rewarded them with success. Such appeasement will not motivate them to leave us alone. Rather, it encourages them to try again with other demands. If they get their way by threats and violence once, they will just offer more threats and violence to get their way again and again. What is needed instead is a plan to overcome the danger while continuing to do the work.

The enemies' plots were defused.

The enemies became aware then that Nehemiah and the Jews knew about their plans. They were not going to succeed with surprise attacks, as they had hoped, because the people were protected behind the walls and were on guard. Furthermore, they were prepared to fight and defend their families.

This led the enemies to be the ones who were discouraged. They were apparently unwilling to fight if it required a direct attack on those who were prepared to fight back. Like terrorists, they sought to harm defenseless, unprotected citizens whom they thought would not fight back. So they did not attack at all!

As a result, the people were able to return to working on the wall. It appears that initially the work was discontinued as the people prepared for defense against the enemies. But once it became apparent that the enemies would not attack as long as the people were prepared for defense, they could return to the work.

Note that God was given credit for bringing the plot of the enemies to nothing. This was God's answer to their prayers. (Compare Job 5:12.)

We need similar plans today.

As already discussed, we do not fight physical battles in God's service today (see v8). But we need similar strength and courage in our spiritual battles. We should not be afraid but remember that we are doing God's work. So if we trust and pray to Him, He will work and fight for us, just as He has always done for His faithful servants.

Likewise, we need to be concerned enough for our families that we are willing to fight the spiritual battles required by opposition to sin. We must never allow temptation, false doctrine, and especially the forces of evil in the world to take our family members into sin without a fight! We must take out the armor of God and the sword of the spirit and fight the good fight of faith!

Family members must decide for themselves whether or not to faithfully serve God, but let them never leave the faith without a fight on our part to save them from sin! We cannot be certain that no family member will ever be lost to Satan; they are free moral agents. But diligent effort and courageous spiritual warfare will defeat him if our loved ones truly want to serve the Lord.

4:16-18 – The workers remained armed as they worked.

Although the enemies' initial plots had been defused, the very nature of such plots is that they demanded God's people to be always on guard. Had the Jews discontinued their vigilance, the enemies could simply proceed with their original plans. So Nehemiah made ongoing provisions for the people to be protected even as the work continued. They were now convinced that they could return to the work, but they also had to provide defense as they worked. Both were now needed.

From that time on, half of Nehemiah's servants worked on the wall, while the other half continued armed and ready for battle. (This appears to me to refer, not to the people in general, but to Nehemiah's own special servants – note verse 23. The people in general are described in the following verses.) Meanwhile, the leaders continued to give the people support, encouragement, and guidance.

When workers carried burdens, they arranged their loads so that they carried with one hand and kept a weapon in the other hand. As they did construction work on the wall itself, people were also armed, having a sword or weapon with them at all times.

Meanwhile, Nehemiah had a man with him at all times who was prepared to sound a trumpet. We will see his purpose as the description proceeds.

The point of these measures was constant preparation for defense even as the work continued. The danger was not allowed to prevent the work, but the work also did not prevent the defense. Both measures were needed.

4:19-21 – *Trumpets would call people to the place of attack.*

Everyone was armed and prepared for battle. But Nehemiah explained to the leaders and the people that the wall was large, so the workers were widely separated from one another. When an attack came, it would surely occur at some particular point on the wall, not on the whole wall at once. But they could never know where an attack would come. So some means was needed to rally the people to the point of attack, wherever it came.

This is what the man with the trumpet would accomplish (verse 18). The trumpet would warn the people where the attack was occurring, so the people would know to gather there to fight the defense. (We are not told exactly how the trumpeter would indicate where the attack was occurring. Perhaps the choice of notes sounded would indicate the place or perhaps the trumpeter would go to the spot and blow the trumpet there.)

But in any battle that came, they were to remember that God was with them and would fight for them (compare verse 14; Exodus 14:14,25; Deuteronomy 1:30; 3:22; 20:4; Joshua 23:10; 2 Chronicles 20:29).

So in this way "we labored in the work." Half held spears from morning till night, even as the others worked (as on verse 16, I am not sure whether this applied to the people in general or just to Nehemiah's personal servants).

4:22,23 – *People remained in the city at night, and Nehemiah and his men remained vigilant.*

The final descriptions of the provisions included that all the people and their servants were to stay in the city behind the wall at night. One advantage of this was that the people could all serve to protect one another. None would be exposed to special danger by being near the enemies without protection, as the people had feared (verse 12). All would be behind the wall to be protected and to help protect the others. The other advantage was that all were in the city so they could help in the work on the wall during the day.

The diligence of Nehemiah and his servants

Nehemiah, his servants, his brothers (presumably his literal brothers), and his special guard that accompanied him were always on call to meet a need in the city. They never even took off their clothes except to wash (presumably to wash themselves and/or to wash the clothes). This meant they were always ready to respond to any emergency. They would not even have to take time to clothe themselves.

The next chapter tells more about the dedication of Nehemiah and his servants to the work of God.

The need for positive and negative work in the kingdom today

Many lessons can be learned from Nehemiah's efforts to protect the people and deal with their enemies. The most basic one is our need to trust God and pray to Him for care and protection. Another lesson is the need for constant vigilance against enemies.

But a special lesson is that our work for God is both positive and negative. It involves both offense and defense. We must build up God's kingdom (as the Jews built the wall), even as we fight the forces of evil. Our work is neither entirely offensive nor entirely defensive but a combination of both. We must protect the Christians from being taken captive by Satan to sin and destruction, even as we help them grow and help save the lost from sin.

The ultimate goal is positive: we seek to build up the kingdom by helping souls be saved and grow up in Christ. But to achieve this we must also fight against temptation, sin, and false doctrine both within the church and from without. We fight evil, not because we enjoy being negative or combative, but because it is necessary to help people be saved.

And finally note that all people need to be both offensive and defensive. Everyone needs to be prepared to fight against the forces of evil even as he works to grow and to help others to be saved and to grow. This is not the work of just a few. We cannot leave the fighting up to others while we try to be constructive, nor vice-versa. All must be prepared to work in both ways.

Nehemiah Chapter 5

Internal Problems Hinder the Work – Chapter 5

Step #7 in Useful Service to God: Rebuke Sin among God's People.

5:1 – *Conflict developed among the Jews.*

In the midst of the work of building the wall of the city and facing opposition from those outside God's people, Nehemiah had to deal with problems among God's people. People who were Jews, men and their wives, raised a complaint against their Jewish brethren.

Likewise today in our service to God problems will confront us, not just from those who are not God's people, but also sometimes from among those who are God's people. We must deal with problems from within as well as problems from outside.

5:2-5 – *The complaint: Jews were taking unfair advantage of the hardships of other Jews.*

The complaint was that men could not provide enough food for their sons and daughters (verse 2). Some had even mortgaged their fields, vineyards, and houses to get money to buy food, because there had been a famine or drought (verse 3). Some had to borrow money to pay the taxes that the king had levied on fields and vineyards (verse 4).

The end result was that some of them had to sell their own children to be slaves, but then could not redeem them, because other men now controlled their property. Apparently having mortgaged their property, they were not able to pay the interest they were being charged (see subsequent verses). Then when they could not pay, the creditors foreclosed and took the property. This left the people without means to provide income for their families, so they ended up selling them as slaves. Even then they might have some hope of redeeming them (buying them back) from slavery, if they could have a source of income. But as it was, they were in effect losing everything they had to their creditors.

But they said they had the same flesh as their fellow-Jews and had children like theirs. This meant they were all of the same nation, all related to one another as descendants of Jacob. The point of this, we will see, is that Jews were forbidden by the law to charge interest to other Jews, and they could take slaves only for a limited period of time. So the charge was that the creditors were not following the law of God regarding how to treat fellow-Jews in time of need.

The people faced a circumstance where, even above other times, they should have been united, working together in a common cause. Instead, they were taking unfair advantage of unfortunate circumstances others faced. Instead of caring and assisting one another, they sought their own gain at the loss of others.

5:6-13 – *Nehemiah rebuked the Jews and required them to make restitution to those whom they had wronged.*

Nehemiah became very angry when he heard these complaints. Note that anger is not necessarily wrong. In fact, the Bible records many examples especially in which righteous leaders of God's people were very angry when they observed sin in the lives of others. See Psalm 7:11; Exodus 11:4-8; 32:19-24; Numbers 16:15; Mark 3:5; 2 Corinthians 7:11; Ephesians 4:26.

Nehemiah was upset that the people were guilty of sin. Sin should always upset us. No faithful servant of God should be neutral about sin. We should especially be upset when God's people mistreat one another, and especially when it happens at a time when it is so important for people to work together to serve God.

The nature of the sin the people had committed

Many Scriptures forbade what the Jews were doing to one another: See Exodus 21:2-6; 22:25-27; Leviticus 25:13-17,35-38,39-46; Deuteronomy chapter 15; 23:19,20; Ezekiel 22:12.

The law said that children of Israel could not charge interest of other Israelites who became poor. This did not forbid charging interest of people of other nations, nor did it forbid charging interest for loans for other purposes, such as business expansion or personal pleasure, etc. But when an Israelite was in need, fellow-Israelites were to have pity and help them by lending without interest. Clearly this law was being violated by those who were charging interest to the suffering Jews in Nehemiah's day.

Furthermore, the law provided for a needy Jew to sell himself or family members to be slaves in time of need. This too was actually an act of mercy, because the owner then was responsible to provide for the needs of the slave, who otherwise would have no means to provide for his needs. But Israelites could not permanently enslave other Israelites. After seven years, the owner had to let the slave go, unless the slave wanted to stay. Again, this did not apply to slaves of people from other nations, but only to Israelite slaves.

Furthermore, property that was bought from others had to be returned whenever the year of jubilee occurred, once every fifty years. Knowing this was required, when property was sold its value was calculated on the basis of the number of years the buyer could hold it till he had to return it on the year of jubilee.

Obviously, the Jews here in Nehemiah 5 were violating all these commands of the law.

How Nehemiah dealt with the problem

We have seen that he was bothered about the problem. Many people are upset over problems among God's people but do nothing about them. Nehemiah determined to act. What did he do?

We can learn much from his example. What Nehemiah did here is the same basic procedure we should follow when we observe Christians today sin against other Christians.

1. He decided upon a Scriptural plan of action.

He thought about the matter seriously. He studied the matter out and decided how best to proceed. He did not ignore the matter, as many people do. But neither did he fly off half-cocked and act or speak without thinking the matter through first. He thought the matter out carefully before he acted. We should do the same before we attempt to resolve a problem among God's people.

2. He confronted the people and directly stated the charges against them.

He personally rebuked the nobles and rulers who were guilty. He stated his charge against them: they were exacting usury (interest) of their brethren – i.e., fellow-Jews.

Note that he did not gossip behind their backs, as many do. He did not just commiserate with innocent victims. He confronted the guilty. This takes courage, but it is the only way to resolve the problem.

Many people today think we should just overlook problems among God's people. We are told that attempting to deal with them might just stir up more trouble or drive people away. But wrong is wrong. People were suffering, and souls were in danger. Furthermore, sin among God's people also drives people away from God, as we will see. Failing to deal with problems just creates more problems. Nehemiah dealt with the problem by confronting those in sin. We must do the same.

3. He called a meeting of the whole assembly to deal with the sins.

Verse 7 tells us that he confronted those in sin and accused them to their faces, then he called them to account in the presence of the congregational assembly. We are not told of any discussion that occurred with them at that time, though I suppose some must have occurred. In any case, it was appropriate to take this matter before the whole congregation, because the sins of the creditors were widely known. Many people were involved and others knew about it. It was not a private matter to be resolved privately, so Nehemiah called a meeting of the assembly to deal with it.

Likewise today, when some of God's people are known to be guilty of sin, the matter must be resolved before the congregation. If men repent, they must acknowledge it to the congregation. If not, the matter must be taken before the church to be dealt with.

See verses on church discipline for how sin among God's people should be dealt with today: 1 Corinthians 5; 2 Thessalonians 3:6,14,15; Matthew 18:15-17; Titus 3:10,11; Romans 16:17,18; 1 Timothy 1:3-11,19,20; 2 Corinthians 2:6-11; 2 John 9-11; Hebrews 12:15; 1 Corinthians 15:33.

4. He presented his evidence against the men in the presence of the assembly.

He explained how, to the extent they were able, the Jews had just gone to great lengths to redeem their Jewish brethren from slavery in other nations. They had been in captivity in Babylon and elsewhere, but had been allowed to return. With great effort and expense, they had helped one another leave bondage.

Did it make sense to work so hard to help their fellow-Jews escape slavery at the hand of other nations, only to enslave them to other Jews? Jews were enslaving other Jews. It was bad enough if Jews suffered at the hands of other nations. Should they suffer at the hands of one another? Such made no sense, so this showed the error of the creditors.

Those who were guilty had no answer for Nehemiah's arguments. Note the value of reasoning with people in error, confronting them directly, even in the presence of the whole assembly of God's people.

5. Nehemiah explained the bad influence of such conduct.

He reasoned further that such conduct was bad, because it would bring upon them and upon God reproach from their enemies. They all knew they had enemies. They were still in the midst of dealing with those enemies at the end of chapter 4.

When God's people themselves are guilty of sin and mistreating one another, this gives people in sin justifiable grounds to ridicule God and His people. We often hear people today ridicule the sin and hypocrisy among God's people. "Why should I want to be one of them? I'm already as good as they are!"

Many passages warn of the danger that improper conduct among God's people will drive people away from God. See 1 Timothy 4:12; Matthew 5:13-16; 18:6,7; Titus 2:7,8; 1 Peter 2:11,12; 2 Corinthians 6:3; 8:20,21; 1 Corinthians 8:9-13; 10:23-33; 2 Samuel 12:14; Romans 2:24.

Note that this is an argument regarding the importance of proper influence. Sometimes people claim that we need not be concerned for what effect we have on the enemies of truth, because they are lost and don't care about God anyway. But God cares! He does not want these people to have justifiable grounds to reproach Him or His people. And sinful conduct among God's people makes it so much harder for those in sin to be converted to the truth.

6. Nehemiah set a good example.

Nehemiah himself, along with his brothers and his servants, were lending money and grain to the people in need. Obviously they did so without charging interest. So he called on the other creditors to likewise quit charging interest.

Surely Nehemiah did not mean this to be boastful or bragging. The point was that he himself was already showing them the example of what they should do. It was both possible and proper to lend money to those in need without charging interest. This would eliminate the problem. So he directly called on the people to imitate his example and cease charging interest.

Note how important it is, when we face sin and seek to stand for truth, that we ourselves have a clear conscience and a good example. Nehemiah could never have convinced others to cease mistreating others had he himself been guilty. The same applies to us today.

7. He called for repentance and restitution.

Having charged them to discontinue charging interest and no longer do so in the future (verse 10), Nehemiah then demanded that they make restoration of the things they had wrongfully taken: lands, vineyards, olive groves, houses, and the portion of the money and crops that they had charged the people.

Note that there was to be no procrastination. He said to do it "even this day." Correction of sin is urgent.

Many Scriptures teach that, when we have committed sin, we must acknowledge the sin, be sorry for it, and determine to cease committing the sin to be forgiven and please God. That is repentance. See Luke 13:3,5; 24:47; Acts 17:30; Matthew 21:28-32; Acts 2:38; 3:19; 5:31; 20:21; 2 Peter 3:9; 2 Corinthians 7:10; Acts 8:22; Matthew 6:12; 21:28-32; 1 John 1:8-10; Proverbs 28:13.

But it is not enough just to discontinue the sin. To the extent possible we must also correct or overcome the harmful effects caused upon others by the sins we have committed. This is also part of doing the "fruits of repentance." In this case that required returning the property that had been wrongfully taken. See Ezekiel 33:14,15; Leviticus 6:1-5; Ezra 10:3,11,17,19,44; Matthew 21:28-31; Luke 19:8; Philemon 10-14,18,19.

8. He required a definite, stated commitment of exactly what changes would be made.

The sinners stated that they would restore the property and would no longer require of the people that which they had no lawful right to require. In short, they promised to do what Nehemiah had charged them to do. The matter was effectively resolved among God's people, because the sinners agreed to make the necessary corrections. This is the only acceptable solution likewise today, when there is sin among God's people.

Nehemiah then went further and called upon the priests, the spiritual leaders, to put the sinners under oath to make a sacred promise to make the correction they had promised to make. Note that it was not enough just to obtain a general promise to "do better," or a general apology of "I'm sorry." Nehemiah demanded a specific understanding of exactly what correction was required and a definite, stated commitment on the part of the people of exactly what they were going to do to correct the matter.

Such measures are also needed today when people have sinned, especially when Christians have sinned against one another. We should not be satisfied with just a general confession, "I'm sorry if I have wronged anyone." When the wrong is known, the sinner must make specific commitment of exactly what they will do in the future to correct the error. Such an approach helps people know exactly what is agreed upon and exactly what to expect of one another. It gives a definite resolution the problem. And it motivates the sinner to make the change that is needed. If he fails to change, everyone will know because everyone knows what he agreed to do.

9. He emphasized the seriousness of the matter and warned of the consequences of further sin.

To show the seriousness of the need for people to make the promised changes, he shook out the folds of his garment. This symbolized that God would likewise shake out the men if they did not keep their promise to change and make restitution. He would reject them and empty them from their own houses and property.

The people witnessed all this solution, including the commitment and the warning of consequences of failure. As a result of the commitment that had been made, those in sin made the needed correction. In short, the solution worked and resolved the matter.

Step #8 in Useful Service to God: Set a Good Example and Be Willing to Sacrifice.

5:14,15 – Nehemiah did not accept the provisions that had been allotted to the governor.

Nehemiah did not just require others to care for the needy and seek their wellbeing. He had already stated that he did not charge interest when he loaned to people in need. But these next few verses show how he went even beyond that in sacrificing to achieve the cause for which the nation labored.

First, he said that, for twelve years (from the 20th to the 32nd year of the reign of Artaxerxes) he did not take the provisions that the governor had a right to receive (compare verse 18). Here we are plainly told that Nehemiah was the governor at that time.

Former governors had taxed the people requiring that they provide the governor with bread and wine and forty shekels of silver. Even the servants of the former governors had made demands of the people. Nehemiah, however, demanded none of this, because of his fear of God.

There is no evidence that it would have been wrong for Nehemiah to accept such provisions to charge for his services. The laborer is worthy of his hire. But he saw the depressed conditions among God's people (see verse 18), so he did not charge them, apparently having an adequate income from other sources. He practiced what he had preached to the creditors among the Jews, and he even went far beyond what he had required of them.

5:16,17 – Nehemiah himself joined in the work and even provided for the needs of others.

He did not consider himself or his servants to be above joining personally in the work on the wall. Rather he and all his servants gathered and participated in the work.

Some leaders think they are too good to personally dirty their hands with the actual work. They think they should sit and supervise while others sweat and labor. True leaders, however, do not just command others; they lead by example.

Likewise, he did not seek personal gain by accumulating wealth for himself. He did not buy land. No doubt this includes especially not taking the land of those in poverty. But apparently in general he did seek to accumulate personal wealth. Rather, he sacrificed so the work could go on and the people not suffer.

We too need to sacrifice for the good of God's work and concentrate on getting the work done in the best way, not trying to accumulate personal gain.

Besides providing for himself and his servants, without taking provisions from the people, Nehemiah used his own provisions to provide for one hundred fifty people who were Jews and rulers. They all sat at his table. He fed them, and perhaps even housed them. And this did not count people whom, as governor, he entertained from surrounding nations.

We are not told what sources of income he used to do this. He had evidently been prominent in Persia, so perhaps he had accumulated some wealth. Or perhaps he received income from the king's treasury, instead of from taxing the people. In any case, the point is that he could have used his position to increase his own wealth and prosperity, but instead he used what he had to forward the work.

All this shows Nehemiah's generosity and concern to see God's work prosper. He was willing to make personal sacrifices, labor hard, and provide for others at his own expense, in order to accomplish the work.

5:18,19 – Nehemiah's daily provisions summarized

Providing for all these people required Nehemiah to have prepared one ox and six sheep each day, besides fowl. And every ten days he received an abundance of all kinds of wine (remember that wine is not necessarily alcoholic in the Bible – see notes on 2:1). But in all this he did not require that the people provide for him as governor, because he saw how the people were heavily burdened as it was (see on v14).

Obviously, this provision required an income of some kind, but we are not told what it was. The important point is that he did not take from the people, but gave for the good of the work.

He finishes this description of his efforts on behalf of the work by calling on God to remember all he had done for the good of God's people. He did not expect a reward from the people, but he hoped for reward from God. We should do the same.

What sacrifices have we made to serve God? What have we given up that we might really like to have or do? Many will not even give up personal pleasures, such as sports, entertainment, or recreation, in order to serve God. Some, rather than sacrificing these at times to serve God, actually want the church to provide more of such things for them!

People think, "I want it. I enjoy it. Why should I give it up?" So we persist in pleasing self at the cost of practicing immorality or causing a brother to stumble or just failing to sacrifice as we should to accomplish the work God wants done. We need to learn from Nehemiah.

Nehemiah Chapter 6

Opposition Continues Yet the Wall Is Completed – Chapter 6

Third Method of Opposition: Discussion to Achieve Compromise or to Hinder the Work

Chapter 4 had described the first two major efforts of the Jews' opponents to defeat the efforts to build the walls. They had attempted ridicule and plotted violence, but God had blessed Nehemiah and the people to continue the work despite the opposition. Chapter 5 had described internal strife among the Jews that hindered the work, but that had been overcome by urging people to follow God's law.

This chapter describes continued efforts of the enemies to hinder the work. The first of these efforts involved an attempt to get Nehemiah to meet with the enemies.

6:1,2 – *The enemies proposed a meeting but intended to do harm to Nehemiah.*

These verses tell us that the work on the wall was progressing well, to the point that the wall no longer had any breaks in it. The entire wall was joined together; however, the doors had not yet been hung at the gates. The people were accomplishing the work despite the problems and hindrances.

This success was reported to Sanballat, Tobiah, and Geshem. These men had opposed Nehemiah's work for God since the beginning. Note that verse 1 expressly calls them enemies. They had ridiculed the work, accused the Jews of violating the king's commands, and threatened to stop the work by violence (2:10,19; 4:1-9; compare 6:5-14). They had been shown their error but continued opposing the work (2:20).

Here they continued their opposition, but using a different tactic. They demanded that Nehemiah meet with them in one of the villages on the plain of Ono to discuss. But their intent was to harm him (verse 2). They did not really want to repent, admit their error, or even discuss to consider the possibility that they might be wrong. Presumably they sought to take Nehemiah captive or even kill him, so the work would be forced to end.

6:3,4 – Nehemiah refused to leave the work to meet.

Nehemiah sent messengers saying that he was doing an important work and would not leave it to talk with them.

Note that Nehemiah refused because:

1) These men had consistently shown they were opposed to the work that God wanted done.

2) They had been rebuked, but continued in error.

3) They had previously tried to harm Nehemiah, and they called for this discussion for the purpose of harming him. We are not told how Nehemiah knew this, but their past conduct proved it. Perhaps he had other sources of information besides.

4) To meet with them would accomplish no good but would hinder Nehemiah from doing the work God wanted done.

These men sent similar messages to Nehemiah four separate times, but Nehemiah consistently refused to meet. He always answered them in the same way. Note that people who oppose God's work are often persistent. They continue to try to prevent the work. Sometimes they think they can badger God's people into giving in. But Nehemiah was also persistent. He refused to give in.

Lessons for us to learn

Many Scriptures teach that we should be willing to meet with people in error to try to help them learn the truth and change their lives. See Jude 3,4; 1 Peter 3:15; Mark 12:28; Acts 17:2,3,17; 2 Timothy 4:2-4; Luke 17:3; etc.

However, from passages like this one in Nehemiah we also learn that our obligation in such matters is limited. There are times when it is unprofitable, dangerous, or even wrong to meet with some people under some circumstances. See also Nehemiah 6:1-9; Matthew 7:6; 21:23-32; 26:59-63; 27:12-14; John 19:9; Luke 23:7-10; 1 Timothy 1:3-7; 6:3-5; 2 Timothy 2:14-18; Titus 3:9-11.

Based on the above Scriptures, we can learn there are two cases in which we should refuse to discuss with people or answer their questions:

1) Some questions should not be allowed to become a cause for strife regardless of who asks them.

Some subjects have no practical value or profit in helping anyone be saved eternally, but will only lead to strife, argument, conflict, and division.

Examples may include:

* Arguments over technicalities of genealogies. A person's ancestry has nothing to do with salvation under the gospel.

* Arguments about technicalities of Old Testament law. That law is no longer in effect. Studying it can benefit our understanding of the nature of God and His will for today. But unless a discussion has some value for our lives today, we should avoid becoming embroiled in disputes.

* Arguments about technicalities of the nature of angels and other spirit beings: How many angels can sit on the head of a pin?

* Speculations about hypothetical issues that have no practical value in our lives and in no way affect our eternal destiny. Can God create a mountain so huge He cannot move it? Could God create people on another solar system, and if so must they obey the same commands we do to be saved?

Many other examples could be cited, many of them not as obvious as these. Judgment is involved in individual cases, and we may differ regarding how far to go in a discussion before we realize it is unworthy of discussion. Nevertheless, the principles are valid and should be remembered. Such topics should not be discussed to the point of strife no matter how sincere the people may be who want to discuss them. Rather, we should point out that the topics have no value to saving anyone's soul but cause strife and division. Then we should turn the conversation to topics that are essential to salvation.

2) Some people have proved themselves to be unworthy of further teaching even on valuable topics.

Even when topics do have practical value in serving God, we should refuse to discuss with some people. When they have had abundant opportunity to know the truth but reject it while teaching false doctrine, and especially when they use whatever we say as an opportunity to attack and slander us, we should drop the discussion and move on.

Such people may try to intimidate and pressure us into answering their questions or discussing with them. They may accuse us of having something to hide or not being able to answer. But nothing good will come of such discussions except strife, anger, division, and pain.

Often, but not always, these two cases occur together.

People who reject the truth will often look for opportunities to ensnare or trap us. They will go to lengths to make up hypothetical speculative cases to argue about. We should refuse such discussions for both the reasons we have studied.

Some people and some questions do not deserve to be answered. The only thing that will come from it is prolonging of strife and division, and like swine people will use the opportunity to turn and rend you.

Fourth Method of Opposition: Make Accusations that Impugn Motives and Attitudes.

6:5-7 – Sanballat wrote a letter accusing Nehemiah of rebelling and seeking to make himself king.

When the four attempts to compel Nehemiah to meet failed, Sanballat did not give up. Like other enemies of the truth, he moved on to another tactic. He wrote still another letter to Nehemiah. This time, however, it was an open letter. That is, it was not confidential or personal for Nehemiah. Rather, it was written with the intent of circulating it to make other people aware of accusations against Nehemiah.

The letter claimed that the news was being spread, even among people of other nations, that Nehemiah and the Jews were planning to rebel against the government. No proof was offered; in fact the letter admits these were rumors. But Geshem was cited as the source of this accusation. Geshem, of course, was one of Sanballat's companions in opposing the work (compare 2:19). He could hardly be classed as an unbiased witness. And no evidence is given as the basis for his accusations.

They claimed further that Nehemiah wanted to become king, and the real purpose of the wall was to begin a military buildup so he could succeed in a revolt. They further claimed that Nehemiah had appointed prophets for the express purpose of teaching the people that Nehemiah would be king in Judah.

The letter threatened that all this would be reported to the king of Persia, unless Nehemiah agreed to meet with them about this. This seems to be a threat that if he did not agree to meet, then they would pass on this report to the king. Perhaps they were also pretending that they could help avoid consequence for Nehemiah if he would consult with them, but either way the effect is that of a threat.

Note that, when enemies fail in their requests to meet with God's people (with the intent of using the results to hurt them), the next step is to threaten and accuse as a means of pressuring for a meeting. This includes making false accusations to discredit the reputation of the workers, so they will feel the need to meet to protect their reputation. And if they don't meet, then the accusations against them will be circulated and allowed to stand. However, all this was done on the basis of accusations that were mere rumors without a shred of evidence offered to support them. Anyone can make accusations. Geshem did so, but there was no proof.

6:8,9 – Nehemiah denied the accusations saying the people were simply trying to hinder the work.

Nehemiah denied the accusation and said the enemies had made it up without proof.

Nehemiah dealt with the false accusations simply by issuing a statement that the accusations were false. The things he was accused of were not being done. Then he said where the ideas came from: the enemies had invented them in their own hearts.

In short he pointed out that there was no proof. Anybody can make accusations. Faithful servants of God have throughout history been accused of all kinds of things that they had never done. But accusations do not constitute proof.

Accusations are likewise made against God's true servants today. We are accused of being motivated by a desire for money, power, or influence. We are said to be jealous or self-righteous, and want to exalt ourselves. We are said to be negative, critical people, condemning and judging others in violation of Scripture, "antis," etc. Or we are accused of being motivated by "hate": we just have something personal against people or want to get rid of them.

Nehemiah simply denied the charges and affirmed the people had made them up without proof. Then since no proof had been offered, he continued with the work. Note that he did not go to meet with the enemies, nor did he stop the work. He did not allow unproved accusations to intimidate him into meeting with the false accusers or into hindering the work God had given him.

He kept his focus on the real root cause of the conflict.

He realized that the real motive behind all these accusations and the efforts to get meetings was to make him afraid so he would stop the work. The enemies were using a psychological ploy. The goal was to get the Jews to think that, if they kept working, these charges would be reported to the king and the people might get in trouble even if the charges could not be proved. But it they would stop the work, then the enemies would stop the accusations, would not report them to the king, etc. So the temptation is to stop simply because of the intimidation and fear of reprisals, not because there was any truth to the charges.

Note that Nehemiah not only did not take the bait to meet with the enemies, but he kept his focus on the real issues involved. The enemies could not prove their accusations against him. But even more important, they did not really care about those accusations. The real concern on their part was not whether or not Nehemiah would rebel against the king. Their real concern was that the wall was being built, and they wanted to stop it.

This shows another important principle of dealing with false accusation: Keep the focus on the real root cause of the conflict. Do not be distracted into discussions of secondary issues. If false accusations are made, just deny them. But keep your focus on the real root issue. Doing this helps us overcome the temptation to be intimidated and back off from the really important issue.

He prayed to God for strength.

Not only did he keep working, but he prayed to God to give him strength to endure the hardship and to keep on with the work. This is exactly what we need to do when we face such false accusations.

Remember that God is the one we ultimately seek to please. If we cease doing His will in order to have peace with men, then we have displeased the One whom we really ought to please. He is the one who gave us orders, and He is the one who can give us strength to prevail. Trust Him and keep His will foremost.

Fifth Method of Opposition: Tempt Leaders to Sin or Fear so as to Discredit Them.

6:10,11 – Nehemiah was tempted to hide in the temple to save his life, but he refused.

The next effort to hinder and discredit Nehemiah's work came from a man named Shemaiah. This man was a secret informer. The ASV says he was "shut up." The two translations are hard to reconcile. Nehemiah went to his house. Perhaps Shemaiah had to some extent barricaded himself as a way of showing fear and thereby motivating Nehemiah to do likewise. In any case, "secret informer" seems to express the context best in that he attempted to give Nehemiah secret advice.

He said the two of them should meet and hide in the temple. They should close the doors and barricade themselves in (perhaps like Shemaiah was in his home) for safety from enemies. He secretly informed Nehemiah that the enemies had plotted to kill him. They would come at night to kill him, so the thing to do was to hide for protection in the temple.

Nehemiah argued that one in his position should not show such fear. He should not flee and he should not go into the temple to save his own life. So he refused to go in.

Verse 13 will show that such an act would be a perversion of the purpose of the temple and a violation of its sanctity. Only priests should enter there. Perhaps there were porches where other people could go, but remember that Jesus later cast people out of the temple for using it for purposes other than worship and prayer. To use it for personal protection would be disrespectful to its purpose.

Also showing cowardice to flee and hide would be a hindrance to the work. Nehemiah could not effectively work from a place of hiding. And if the people saw him being so cowardly, they too might become fearful and hide to protect themselves, instead of working. In short, this was another attempt to hinder the work and get Nehemiah to stop working.

We need to remember that sin is wrong in and of itself, even when done for personal protection from persecution. And when we try to do right but allow people to intimidate us to sin or to be disrespectful or cowardly, then we allow them to discredit our work and defeat our efforts for good.

Note that fleeing in and of itself is not sinful. New Testament apostles, preachers, and Christians often fled for safety. But they did not stop their work of preaching the gospel. To allow fear to lead us to stop working for God is the problem.

6:12-14 – Nehemiah realized the enemies had hired a false teacher to make him afraid.

Nehemiah then realized that the man had not been giving him advice from God or in harmony with God's will. Rather, he pronounced this as a prophecy, but he had been hired by Tobiah and Sanballat, the enemies of God's work.

This implies that Shemaiah had presented this as something God would have Nehemiah do, or perhaps even something that God had revealed by prophecy (compare verse 14). This shows the danger of following messages that claim to be from God, if those messages actually contradict God's will.

It also shows that many false teachers are teaching for hire. They have been paid by people to teach as they do.

Had Nehemiah taken the advice, he would have sinned and subjected himself and his work to reproach.

Nehemiah realized that Shemaiah had been hired to tempt Nehemiah to be afraid, hide in the temple, and sin. Then the enemies would have cause to send out an evil report, that they might reproach him. That is, they could discredit him for his sin and cowardice.

As discussed on verses 10,11, had Nehemiah listened to this advice, he would have shown cowardice, neglected the work, and misused the purpose of the temple. This would have been sin (though it does not directly say which part of this was sin or whether it was all sin).

When people cannot intimidate God's people to stop working for God, they often try to discredit us so other people will not listen to us or follow the teaching. They may try to do this by false accusation (as in the previous verses). If that does not work, then they try to get us to actually sin, so they can have grounds to accuse and discredit us. Compare the story of Balaam and Balak (see Revelation 2:14).

This shows the need for courage and a pure life on the part of God's people, especially the leaders. We need to avoid sin, even in the face of false teaching, temptation, threats, and intimidation. We can be sure that people in sin will use everything they can think of against us, so we must give them no ammunition. To fail to live pure lives will discredit our work and hinder God's purpose.

Again, Nehemiah prayed to God to deal with his enemies.

Nehemiah was clearly a man of prayer, and he saw the value of prayer in times of temptation and opposition. He repeatedly turned to God in prayer for strength to deal with the enemies.

He asked God to remember the sinful acts of Tobiah and Sanballat. Also he said a prophetess named Noadiah and other prophets were involved in the attempt to make him afraid. This clearly indicates that more than just one man was involved in the temptation of Nehemiah, and that the attempt did involve the use of prophecy to try to frighten him.

And note too that it is not wrong to call upon God to bring justice and punishment on evildoers. We may not take personal vengeance, but we should leave vengeance to God. It is appropriate for us to remind God that such people do deserve His punishment.

6:15,16 – The wall was completed, causing great discouragement to the enemies.

Despite the best efforts of the enemies, the work continued till the wall was finished. It was completed on the twenty-fifth day of the month Elul. It took a total of fifty-two days. To complete the wall at all was amazing. To complete it under conditions of such opposition is doubly amazing. To do it in fifty-two days is almost incredible. Yet that is what happened.

God has not promised that serving Him will be easy. On the contrary, He has promised there will be opposition and persecution. But He has also promised that we can be successful if we remain faithful despite the opposition and persecution.

The enemies were discouraged by this result.

When the enemies and surrounding nations heard that the wall was completed, they were discouraged. Note that this shows the real motivation for the opposition. Sanballat and his cronies were leaders of opposition by the nations in general. They did not act alone; many people did not want the wall built, because they belonged to enemy nations. They did not want the Jews to be established or become strong. This was the real issue.

When the Jews succeeded, this caused great discouragement to the enemies. They were disheartened. And they realized that the work had been the result of God's own blessing.

Sixth Method of Opposition: Influence God's People to Justify Those Who Are in Sin.

6:17-19 – Jewish nobles communicated with the enemies and spoke favorably of them to Nehemiah.

Tobiah was one of those in league with Sanballat (2:10; 4:3; 6:19; etc.). But Nehemiah reveals that he was communicating regularly with many influential people among the Jews. Many letters were being passed back and forth. The Jews should have been helping in the work on the wall and encouraging those who were working. But meanwhile they were communicating with the enemy, and we will see that they became an influence against the work.

It turns out that Tobiah was married to a daughter of an influential Jew named Shechaniah, whose genealogy is given in the verse (compare 13:4). And also Tobiah's son Jehohanan was married to the daughter of another influential Jew named Meshullam. This Meshullam is listed in Nehemiah 3:4 as being one of those who ought to be working on the wall (compare 8:4). Yet they were allied by marriage to one of the enemies and were as a result "pledged" to him. This surely means they were in league with him. They were trying to help his cause, as shown in v19.

This shows the danger of intermarriage and the power of having a close relationship with those who are in sin. Interestingly, Ezra 10:15 lists a Meshullam as being among those who opposed Ezra's efforts to bring repentance and correction among the Jews who had intermarried with people of the land. This might be another man with the same name, but the similarity of circumstances might be more than mere coincidence. If both passages refer to the same individual, this helps explain all the more the problem caused by intermarriage to people in sin.

Agents among God's people fraternizing and working for the enemy

Specifically, these people became Tobiah's agents working from within God's people. They were numbered among God's people, but they spoke well of Tobiah to Nehemiah, trying to convince him that Tobiah was doing good.

Meanwhile, they also served as a source of information to Tobiah to tell him what Nehemiah was doing. This amounted to being spies or a source of intelligence within the Jews' camp to inform the enemy what was going on.

Meanwhile, Tobiah himself wrote letters to Nehemiah to try to frighten him. What these letters said we are not specifically told. Perhaps they go along with the threats recorded earlier in this chapter and in chapter 4. Presumably they made use of the information Tobiah had obtained from among the Jews.

In any case, while we are not told exactly what Nehemiah tried to do about these Jews in league with Tobiah, still it was clearly a problem. It shows the danger of those who try to be among God's people but are compromisers.

Today, in virtually every case in which God's people have conflict with those in error, there will be some who seek to hold a middle-ground position. They want to speak well of people on both sides. But especially they try to convince those who are taking a firm stand against sin that the people in sin are really not so bad. They speak well of them, talk about their sincerity and good works, and try to say we should not oppose them. They try to bring about compromise and discourage a firm stand against sin.

In many cases such people are a problem as big or bigger than the enemy. We must teach them the truth and give them time to see the truth. But if they continue to sympathize with the enemy, then they become like the enemy and must be dealt with accordingly. See Scriptures on fellowship with sin: 2 John 9-11; Ephesians 5:11; Proverbs 17:15; 2 Corinthians 6:17-7:1; 1 Timothy 5:22; Psalms 1:1,2; 1 Corinthians 15:33; Romans 1:32; Acts 7:58; 8:1; 22:20.

Nehemiah Chapter 7

7:1,2 – Responsibilities assigned and organized

The wall was now complete, doors set in place, etc. Various responsibilities were assigned. Porters or gatekeepers might be compared to modern security guards — perhaps to keep unauthorized people from going where they should not (see verse 3 below).

Singers were part of the worship appointed by David (1 Chronicles 25:1; 2 Chronicles 35:15). Levites were responsible to care for the temple and the ceremonies there, etc.

As governor of Judah (5:14; 8:9), Nehemiah had the authority to delegate responsibilities to men of his choosing. He chose his brother Hanani (compare 1:2) to be in charge of the city of Jerusalem, and also another man named Hananiah to be in charge of the citadel (castle — perhaps this was a responsibility for military leadership, or of the governor's headquarters).

He chose Hanani because he possessed faithfulness and fear (respect) for God more so than others did. Such qualities need to also be considered seriously in people we chose for jobs.

7:3,4 – Gates were closed for protection.

Those responsible for the city were charged to keep the doors closed all night and into the day until the sun was hot. Guards were appointed even though the wall was now complete. They were to stand guard and make sure the doors were shut and barred. Some stood at watch stations and others guarded near their own houses. (The fact they stood guard near where they and their family lived would motivate them to be diligent in their duties.)

These precautions were needed because it was such a large city, but only relatively few people lived there. Presumably they were still concerned about the possibility of attack from their opponents (chapter 4).

7:5,6 – Genealogy was found for the first group who returned from captivity.

God then informed Nehemiah to gather the leaders and the people to make a current genealogy. In doing this, Nehemiah discovered a genealogy from the first group that returned, and it is recorded here. Compare it to the one given in Ezra 2.

Genealogies were important to Israel in determining property rights to the land, and also to determine who could participate in various offices, especially the priests and Levites, who had to be of certain lineage. Most important was the fact that God had promised that the Christ would be a descendant of Abraham, David, etc. The nation of Israel continued and its lineage was kept, so this promise could yet be fulfilled.

What follows is a genealogy of people who returned from captivity after Nebuchadnezzar the king of Babylon had carried them away. Under the leadership of Zerubbabel they returned to Jerusalem and Judah, everyone to his own city.

7:7-69 – *Genealogy of the people who came from Babylon*

These verses list the genealogy of people who had come from Babylon. Note in verses 61-65 certain men could **not** prove by genealogy that they were Israelites, so they were not permitted to serve as priests, nor to eat of the holy things of priests. See notes on Ezra 2:61-63 for further discussion. We will not repeat the information here.

7:70-73 – *Financial contributions to the work*

These verses list various financial contributions made. Some were made by heads of households, others by the governor himself, and others by the rest of the people.

The result was that the people of Israel dwelt in their cities: the priests, Levites, gatekeepers, singers, and Nethinim. See on Ezra 8:20 regarding the Nethinim.

This was the condition of the people in the land when the seventh month of the year began. This was a very special month in the Israelite calendar, because it included various feast days. The next chapter will record some events of their activities on this special month after the wall had been completed.

Part 2: Spiritual Restoration of the People – Chapter 8-13

Nehemiah Chapter 8

Teaching the Law and Keeping the Feast of Tabernacles – Chapter 8

Step #9 in Useful Service to God: Restore God's Service by Teaching People His word.

8:1-3 – The people gathered for the reading of the law.

Now that the wall was completed, the people turned to restoring their spiritual service in the city. The law had commanded that the law be read to the people from time to time (Deuteronomy 3:11,12; Joshua 8:34,35; 2 Kings 23:2).

They assembled in a convenient place described as the open square in front of the Water Gate. The reading was led by Ezra the scribe, the same Ezra described in the book of Ezra (see on Ezra 7:6). Ezra had led the second group that returned from captivity, and Nehemiah led the third group. Evidently these were not far apart.

Ezra brought the book of the law and read from it from morning till noon. The message is called the Book of the Law of Moses that the Lord had commanded Moses. Note the clear claim that Moses' writings were inspired by God. See also the notes on v8, where the law is called the Law of God.

Those who were assembled were men, women, and all who could hear and understand what was taught. The people listened attentively to what was read. This occurred on the first day of the 7th month, which was a holy day (verse 9), the feast of trumpets (see verses 14ff).

Note the value of reading God's written instructions.

We today also need to read God's law. In those days before the printing press, copies were hard to come by, so the law was read publicly. New Testament examples record it being read regularly in the synagogues. We should also read it, and we have the advantage that we can easily possess our own copies. This is the value of having the word in writing, but we must realize the value of reading and studying it.

The people paid attention. We should do the same. Attention is hindered by daydreaming, whispering, joking, playing with babies, etc. Note that, even though the session was lengthy (morning till midday), people still were attentive. They did not complain that they could not absorb any more after a certain length of time, as some complain today. If they could listen and benefit for that long, why can't we?

8:4-6 – The pattern of the reading

An elevated platform had been built so the people could see (and presumably hear) Ezra. With him were various other men named here who helped the people understand (see also verses 7,8).

When Ezra praised God, the people said "Amen!" This is an expression of agreement meaning "so be it." It affirms that the hearer agrees that the message spoken is true. It is appropriate for the audience to express "Amen" to the words spoken, provided it is a genuine expression of agreement. It should not be allowed to be done to the point of distracting from the message or simply to drum up excitement. See Nehemiah 5:13; 1 Corinthians 14:16.

We are told that the people stood when he opened the book. When Ezra praised God, the people lifted their hands and bowed their faces toward the ground. This is acceptable posture for worship, but it is surely not the only permissible posture. Many other postures are described in Scripture. What matters is that the acts done in worship be authorized by God and sincerely meant from the heart. Specific posture is not required, though some positions at some time may help us concentrate or express our meaning.

8:7,8 – Leaders read the law and explained the meaning.

Other men are named as assisting in the teaching. The people stood in their place, and these men helped them understand the law as it was read. They did this by explaining the meaning to the people.

This is the plain simple essence of gospel teaching and preaching. Proper teaching requires appeal to the book as the source or basis of our teaching and our only authority. We should not use human ideas as our foundation. Then we help people understand what it says by explaining the meaning. Note that God authorizes helping people understand the meaning of Scripture. What is not authorized is changing the meaning or adding our own human ideas that differ from it.

Note that the people did understand the meaning – note especially verse 12. Understanding the written word is not impossible nor is it reserved for specially trained leaders. The common person can understand it but must work hard at studying and learning.

Note also that, comparing verse 1 to verse 8 shows that the "law of Moses" and the "law of God" are the same thing. There is no difference as some claim. The terms are interchangeable, because God gave the law, but He gave it through Moses — verse 1. Some claim that the Law of Moses is the ceremonial law and was removed when Jesus died, but they claim the Law of God is the Moral Law or Ten Commands, which remains in effect today. Passages like this show the error of such distinctions. See also notes on Ezra 7:6.

8:9-12 – *The people wept when they heard the law, but the leaders said it should be a time of rejoicing.*

When the people heard the law, they wept. There are many reasons for weeping when one hears God's law. This was especially the case of these people, who had not been able to worship as they would have liked to, because the city of worship had been so destroyed. We weep when we have godly sorrow for our sin (as in chapter 7; compare 2 Corinthians 7:10), or when we appreciate how good God has been and how unworthy we are, etc.

However, Nehemiah, Ezra, and the other leaders who were teaching the people told them not to weep. It was not a day for weeping, but was a time for joy. It was a holy day, the Feast of Trumpets – compare verse 2 to Leviticus 23:24. This was expressly commanded to be a time for eating and drinking, and giving food to those who were had none – Deuteronomy 16:14; compare Deuteronomy 26:11-13; Esther 9:19,22. The people did as told.

Note that the passage expressly says that the people understood the message (compare verse 8). We too can understand if we study honestly and diligently. Those who claim that the Bible cannot be understood are mistaken. See also Mark 7:14; 2 Timothy 3:15-17; Acts 17:11; Ephesians 3:3-5; 5:17; 1 Corinthians 14:33; Isaiah 55:11; Psalm 119:104,105,130; 1 Timothy 2:4.

8:13-15 – *The people prepared to keep the Feast of the Tabernacles.*

On the next day there was another meeting to read the law, the heads of the houses this time meeting with Ezra, the priests, and the

Levites. Note that one day of reading and studying the law was not enough. In fact, we will see that they met together to read and study the law all week long during the Feast of Tabernacles. This is similar to what we would call a gospel meeting. It was a special concentrated time of reading and studying God's law.

As they studied, they read the Scriptures where God revealed that, in the 7th month, there should also be another feast, the Feast of Tabernacles or booths. This is mentioned in Lev. 23:33-44 (Deuteronomy 16:13-17; compare Nehemiah 8:14ff). This feast began on the 15th day of the 7th month and lasted for seven days. The people were to get branches from various trees (olive, myrtle, palm, etc.) to make booths (temporary dwelling places). This was a reminder of the time when they were dwelling in temporary dwelling places in the wilderness after they left Egypt. Many offerings were associated with each day of the Feast of Tabernacles, as listed in Numbers 29:12-38.

8:16-18 – The people kept the Feast of Tabernacles.

Having read the command of the law, the people obeyed. They built booths on the roofs of their houses, or in courtyards, or in the open square before the gates. All the people participated.

The result was that the feast was kept as it had not been since the time of Joshua. This might appear to mean that this feast had not been kept at all since Joshua's time, but that would appear to contradict 2 Chronicles 8:12,13; Ezra 3:4; etc. So another possibility is that the statement could mean no one kept it **in this way** since the time of Joshua (note "so").

Since these people had recently come out of Babylonian captivity, perhaps this feast had special meaning to them as they identified with their fathers who came out of Egyptian captivity. In any case, it was a time of great gladness, which was what God had commanded at this feast (see on verses 9-12 above).

The feast lasted seven days, and on each day the people continued to read the law. On the eighth day they had a special assembly as was commanded for this feast. Note how they continued to want to read and study the law. If they could study for hours per day for a week, surely we can study for a few hours on the first day of the week and other times as well.

Restoration of God's service

Compare Ezra 6:19-22.

Note that the people here restored an act of service to God that had been neglected for years. When we see how they restored it, we will understand the principle of restoration according to the written word. We will see how we can restore all aspects of our service to God as they were in the New Testament, even though it may have been many generations since others did it properly. This requires:

1. The people followed the source of guidance for knowing God's will: the written word.

Note that Moses' words had been written a thousand years earlier and had been neglected for many years at a time in the interim. Yet by diligently studying and following it, the people were still able to restore their service. We can do the same today, despite the fact it has been two thousand years since the New Testament was completed, and despite the fact people have been in apostasy for years at times since then.

2. To help understand, teachers assembled the people, read the law, and explained the meaning of it.

We need teachers today who will show the same dedication.

3. People attended the assemblies and listened attentively.

Restoration today likewise requires the people to have the same commitment and willingness to learn.

4. The people were thus able to understand the written word which they studied.

People often tell us that the Bible was written hundreds of years ago so we can't understand it, and besides it is out of date and has no application today. Yet the same things would have applied in Nehemiah's day, but the people could understand and the law did apply. We can do the same today.

5. The people then obeyed what was written, and the worship was restored.

This worked despite the fact the law had been written 1000 years earlier and had been neglected for years. The same will work today. The power is in the seed to make Christians and restore Jesus' church anytime, anywhere. See 1 Peter 1:22-25; Galatians 6:7,8.

Nehemiah Chapter 9

Review of the History of Israel – Chapter 9

Step #10 in Usefulness to God: Lead People to Recognize and Repent of Sin.

9:1-3 – Once again the people assembled, read the law, and confess their sins.

Again on the 24th day of this seventh month, the people were assembled, fasting, and indicating sorrow by wearing sackcloth and dust on their heads. The Feast of Tabernacles in chapter 8 had taken from the 15th through the 22nd day of the month, with the assembly of the eighth day of the feast occurring on the 22nd (Leviticus 23:34ff). This means that this meeting on the 24th must have been a separate voluntary meeting not required by any feast day.

The people separated themselves from foreigners (compare Nehemiah 13:1-3; Ezra chapters 9 & 10; Deuteronomy 23:3-6). This could refer to specific separation from foreign wives, as in Ezra 9 & 10. Or it may mean they did not make alliances with these foreigners. Or perhaps it means in general that they turned away from all evil influences among these people.

The people took one fourth of the day to read the book of the law of God and then another one fourth of the day to confess their sins and worship God. So, they spent half their day in this special voluntary period of worship and study even after they had spent the eight days of the Feast of Tabernacles in reading the law and worshipping (8:18). This shows the zeal and desire of the people to communicate with God. We need such zeal among God's people today. Too many do not want to spend more than an hour a week in worship and study, and many won't do that much.

In particular, confession of sins is vital if we expect God to accept our worship. See Acts 8:22; Matthew 6:12; 21:28-32; 2 Corinthians 7:10; 1 John 1:8-10; Proverbs 28:13. God will not accept worship from those who claim to be His children but who disobey His word and will not repent (1 John 2:15-17; Romans. 12:1,2; James 4:4; etc.).

9:4-15 – *The people praised God's greatness.*

The men named in verses 4,5 led this confession and worship. They stood on the stairs (presumably so people could see and hear them), then cried aloud and led the people in praising God. They called on the people to stand up and bless (praise) the Lord God.

They then began the prayer of confession and praise by honoring God whose name is exalted so high we cannot bless and praise Him highly enough. God's name stands for the Person and all He is. To praise God's name is to praise Him Himself (see 1 Chronicles 29:13; Matthew 6:9).

God is Lord because God is Creator.

God is praised as the only true Lord. He is Lord because He made heaven and the host of heaven (the heavenly bodies), the earth and sea and everything in them. As Creator of all, He deserves the praise and service of all that He created. Note that God's place as God and Ruler is the consequence of His work as Creator. To deny or doubt His power as Creator is to deny or undermine respect for His right to rule. See Genesis chapter 1; Exodus 20:11; Psalm 33:6-9; 102:25; 89:11; 90:2; 104:5-9,24-28; 19:1; 24:1,2; 95:5; 146:6; 136:5-9; 8:3,6-8; 148:5; Jeremiah 10:12; 27:5; John 1:1-3; Acts 14:15; 17:24; Isaiah 42:5; 45:18; 40:26; Hebrews 1:10; 11:3.

He not only **made** everything, but He **preserves** all that He made (Psalms 36:6; Colossians 1:17). He upholds the continued existence of that which He made. If He were to cease willing them to exist, they would all immediately perish. The fact the world continues to stand is proof of God's continued existence, just as the origin of the world is the proof of His authority over all.

The host of heaven (heavenly bodies) worship Him, not in the sense that they consciously, knowingly praise Him as intelligent beings would do, but their very existence shows forth His power and greatness and thereby honor Him.

God's covenant with Abraham

Just as the creation showed reason to praise God, so does the history of His dealings with man, especially the descendants of Abraham. So the people praised God for the great things done for their ancestors, starting with Abraham. Throughout their history, Jews have loved to recount the story of Abraham and God's subsequent blessings to him. This is the basis for their claim to be God's special people, which indeed they were during the Old Testament.

God chose Abraham and called him out of the land of Ur and brought him to the land of Canaan (Genesis 11:31; 12:1ff). Because of Abraham's faithfulness (Genesis 15:6; chapter 22, especially verse 16), God changed his name to Abraham, meaning a father of many nations (Genesis 17:5). God made the covenant with him (Genesis 15:18-21) to give to his descendants the land of Canaan, including the territory of all the nations specified – these are the same nations repeatedly specified as occupying the territory God would give Israel.

Because God is righteous, He performed these words. This clearly means that the Israelites received the land God promised. This was done in the past – i.e., prior to Nehemiah 9; it was not something to happen yet in the future. See also verses 23,24; Joshu 21:43-45; 23:14. This proves the error of modern premillennialists, who claim Israel still has not received the land fully, but will receive it at Jesus' second coming. The consequence of this view, according to the context here, is that **God is not righteous**!

For further information, see our articles about premillennialism at our Bible Instruction web site at **www.gospelway.com/instruct/**.

God delivered Israel from Egyptian bondage.

As time passed, God also blessed the Israelites who had been captives in Egypt. He saw their affliction and heard their cry (Exodus 2:22-25; 3:7). God performed great wonders against Pharaoh and all the Egyptians (the 10 plagues – Exodus chapter 7-14). He did this because they had acted proudly against Him, thinking He could not overpower them. By His great miracles, He made a name for Himself (Jeremiah 32:20).

So God led the people from captivity. He parted the Red Sea so the people passed through on dry land, but the enemies were destroyed (Exodus 14:20-31). He then led them by pillar of cloud by day and fire by night (Exodus 13:21,22).

All this showed God's power and exalted His name before the world. And all this gave Israel great reason to honor and serve Him. But we will see that they were not faithful, which is the ultimate point of this history.

God gave Israel the law and provided for them in the wilderness.

God then revealed His law to the people at Mt. Sinai (Exodus 19,20), a good and just law (Romans 7:12). This law included the Sabbath (Exodus 16:23; 20:8-11; 23:12; 31:13-17; compare Genesis 2:3) and other precepts and statutes given through Moses. God also fed them with manna in the wilderness (Exodus 16), and gave them water from the rock (Exodus 17:6; Numbers 20:8-11). He led them to the land

He had sworn to give them and told them to go in to possess it (Deuteronomy 1:8; Numbers 13,14).

The expression "made known" surely seems to imply that the people had not known the Sabbath prior to the giving of the law, at least it was not revealed prior to that time that the people were to observe it. The first time we read of people being told to observe the Sabbath was regarding the gathering of manna (Exodus 16). Though this happened shortly before their arrival at Mt. Sinai, it was in the wilderness near to Sinai (Exodus 16:1) and the context probably refers to the whole period in which God gave the law.

If this is the correct conclusion, then God rested on the seventh day of creation and that is the reason He hallowed it (Gen. 2:3), but it was not till later at Mt. Sinai that He revealed that man should keep it. In any case, it is clear from the passages listed above that He addressed the command specifically to the nation of Israel. No one else has ever been required to keep the Sabbath, and no one is required to keep it now that the Old Testament has been removed (Hebrews 10:1-10; 7:11-14; 8:6-13; 9:1-4; 2 Corinthians 3:6-11; Galatians 3:24,25; 5:1-6; Romans 7:1-7; Ephesians 2:11-16; Colossians 2:13-17).

For further information, see our articles about the old law today at our Bible Instruction web site at www.gospelway.com/instruct/.

Summary of God's qualities and works

Note from the things the people have spoken, some of the great qualities of God that the people were praising, and some of the works He has done that prove He has these qualities. We too should praise God in these same ways for these same reasons:

Characteristics	Works
Power	Provision for His people
Wisdom	Creation of universe
Uniqueness (one God)	Preservation of universe
Righteousness	Covenant with Abraham
Faithfulness to promises	Plagues on Egypt
Love, care, & concern	Crossing of Red Sea
Justice	Pillar of cloud/fire
Guidance & authority	Giving of the law
Grace, mercy, & forgiveness	Food & water for Israel
	Israel made a great nation
	Israel given Canaan

9:16-18 – The people of Israel became corrupt.

Having told how great and good God was, the people confessed how corrupt their fathers had been. Their ancestors had acted proudly.

They hardened their necks – i.e., they were stubborn (Deuteronomy 1:26-33; 31:27). They did not obey God's commands and did not remember the good He had done them (Psalm 106:6; 78:11,42-45).

Specifically, they refused to enter the Promised Land, but appointed a leader and wanted to return to Egypt (Numbers 14:4; Acts 7:39). Imagine how offensive this was to God. Here He made such great efforts and did such great miracles to get them out of Egypt to Canaan, and what did the people do when they got there? They refused to enter and wanted to go back to the place He just led them out of!

Consider how this is like some people today. God sent His Son Jesus to die on the cross to lead them out of the curses of sin. And what do the people do? They feel sorry for themselves and think they were better off before they were converted!

Also they worshiped a golden calf saying it was the God that brought them from Egypt (Exodus 32:4-8,31). God did such great things for them, and what did they do? They made an image and attributed all these great works to an idol they made with their own hands. They had committed this great sin even as Moses was on the mountain receiving God's law! Imagine how God must have felt about this!

Yet even so, God was gracious, slow to anger, and abundant in kindness. He did not forsake them despite their sins (Joel 2:13). He punished them and demanded repentance, but He did not destroy them as He had the right to do.

9:19-21 – *God provided for the people in the wilderness.*

Yet for all their evil provocations, God did not completely give up on them, as they deserved (Psalms 106:45). He continued to lead them through the wilderness by the pillar of cloud and fire. He also guided them by the Spirit; this refers to the inspiration of the prophets that taught them – see verse 30; Numbers 11:17.

And despite their sins, He gave them the manna and water for forty years sustaining them as they wandered in the wilderness as punishment for their sins. Their clothes did not wear out and their feet did not swell (Deuteronomy 8:4; 29:5). They had none of the problems you would expect on such a long journey. God provided all they needed.

The contrast is between a righteous God and unrighteous people!

9:22-25 – *God gave Israel the land promised to Abraham.*

God continued to give the people blessings after they wandered in the wilderness. He led them to the promised land and gave them the nations of the people who had been there, beginning with the lands of Sihon, king of Heshbon, and Og, king of Bashan (Numbers 21:21-35).

They became a great nation of many people like the sand of the seashore as promised to Abraham (Genesis 15:5; 22:17; Hebrews 11:12). And again the people plainly state that God did give them the land. We are expressly told that God led them into the land He had told the fathers to go in and possess. So the people went in and possessed the land. God subdued the inhabitants before them and gave Israel the people and the land. See notes on verses 7,8. Again this proves the people did receive the land as promised to Abraham, which in turn disproves premillennialism. Compare Joshua 1:2-4; 18:1; Psalm 44:2,3.

The land was prepared for them to live in without the need for them to work to prepare the land. They took cities, houses, goods, cisterns already dug, vineyards, olives groves, etc. All this happened because of the goodness of God, and the people grew fat (Deuteronomy 32:15) and delighted in that goodness (Hosea 3:5).

9:26 – *Yet the people returned to evil.*

For all God's goodness, the people still disobeyed and rebelled against God and cast the law behind their backs (Judges 2:11; 1 Kings 14:9; Psalm 50:17). What is worse, they even killed the messengers (prophets) God sent to tell them to repent. God knew the people were disobeying Him, He sent warnings, and what did the people do? They killed the messengers!

We are often told of the people doing this (Matthew 23:37; Acts 7:52; 1 Kings 18:4ff; 19:10). We read such records and tend to take it as a matter of course. But imagine being one of the prophets! We get upset if somebody gets mad at us or ceases to be our friend because we talk to them about Jesus. Surely God was greatly provoked.

Compared to God's character and works, as before, note the character and works of the people:

Characteristics	**Works**
Pride	Refused to enter Canaan
Stubbornness	Worshipped the Golden calf
Disobedience	Killed prophets
Ingratitude	

9:27-29 – *God allowed enemies to oppress the people.*

God punished the people by allowing enemies to defeat them (Judges 2:14; Psalm 106:41). They would then repent and God would deliver them (Judges 2:18; Psalm 106:44). But then the people would go back into sin after awhile. So God would leave them in the hands of their oppressors, hoping this would teach them a lesson (Judges 3:12; Psalm 106:43). They would then finally repent and call on God, so He would again show them mercy and deliver them. This was a cycle continually repeated in the times of the judges and kings. Having delivered them from enemies, God warned them to obey, but they refused and stubbornly, proudly refused to listen.

The law requires that, in order to live, one must do what the law said (compare Leviticus 18:5; Gal. 3:12). The wages of sin is death (Ezekiel 18:20; Romans. 6:23; Genesis 2:16f). Often the law required physical death. But even more important is that spiritual death is the consequence of sin. If one wanted to have a relationship with God (often called spiritual life), one had to obey. If he sinned, he was cut off (death).

So under the system of the law, the only way to avoid that death was to live without sin. Even one sin would condemn to death before God. So only those who lived sinlessly could live. But the people repeatedly refused to obey. Again, they shrugged their shoulders, stiffened their necks, and would not listen (see verse 26).

This is the main lesson of the Old Testament. We should not think we are much better. We too sin again and again and need God's patient forgiveness. One main lesson we should learn from these accounts is our own sinfulness and our own need for God's mercy. The law ultimately could not provide forgiveness for the people, so why should we today want to return to that law? We need a system of forgiveness through Jesus. But we also need to learn the importance of obedience and the terribleness of sin.

9:30-32 – *God bore patiently with the people for many years.*

This pattern of rebellion by the people continued for many years. Yet God, in mercy, did not completely destroy the people. He continued to testify to them of their sins by means of the messages sent them by the Holy Spirit through the prophets (see notes on verse 20; 2 Kings 17:13-18; 2 Chronicles 36:11-20; Jeremiah 7:25; Acts 7:51; 1 Peter 1:11; 2 Peter 1:20,21). Note that the Old Testament expressly says that the prophets were guided by God's Holy Spirit. This is confirmed by the New Testament, which then claims the same inspiration for the New Testament apostles and prophets.

Also God continued to deliver them to their enemies. But despite these punishments, God's mercy led Him to continue to spare a remnant of the people. He did not completely consume them, because He is a God of compassion and mercy (Jeremiah 4:27).

The people in Nehemiah's day knew this had happened in ancient times. But it had also happened more recently. Their recent ancestors and rulers had been led to captivity by Assyria and Babylon. So they then called upon God to show mercy upon them and spare them. They urged Him not to consider their needs and troubles to be insignificant. They too needed God's mercy (2 Kings 15:19; 17:3-6; Ezra 4:2,10).

9:33-35 – *The people confessed their own unrighteousness.*

This entire history is summarized in verse 33: God had been just and faithful in dealing with the people, but they had done wickedly

(Psalm 119:137; 106:6; Daniel 9:14,5-8). That in a nutshell is the point of the context. God had repeatedly revealed His will, warned the people, and shown them mercy when they repented. Yet they had repeatedly turned from His will to do evil. That is surely the history of Israel, and even today it is the history of God's people. Let us learn, as they needed to learn, to turn from sin and confess our own errors.

They openly said that their own kings, priests, and ancestors had failed to obey God's law. They had not served God, though He had given them so many good things in the land He gave them. They continued to sin and often would not turn from their sins.

9:36-38 – The people renewed their covenant commitment to serve God.

The people then stood before God as His servants. God had graciously moved the Persians to allow them to return, so they were now back in the land God had given their fathers (Ezra 9:9). They were again enjoying its bounty, even as their fathers had. The land gave its increase.

But the people realized they were not ultimately free to enjoy the blessings of the land. They were still subject to foreign kings (the Persians). Because of their sins, much of the bounty of the land went to the foreign rulers. These rulers had dominion over the people and their animals. So they were in great distress (Deuteronomy 28:33,51,48). Just as their ancestors had suffered at the hands of foreign oppressors and then had repented, so these people were being oppressed and had come to God to confess sin and repent.

But they determined to go further and to renew the covenant with God. They volunteered to make a covenant with God and write it down. Their leaders, the priests and Levites, would lead the people in it and would seal it with official approval. (2 Kings 23:3; 2 Chronicles 29:10; Ezra 10:3; Nehemiah 10:1)

Events in the following chapter describe the sealing of the covenant and the people's commitment to it. So all this was apparently written down as their covenant commitment to return to serving God. Of course, it is written here for us, but it was apparently also written in their day as a reminder of their serious need to serve God.

Nehemiah Chapter 10

The People's Covenant to Serve God – Chapter 10

Step #11 in Useful Service to God: Lead People to Commit Themselves to Obey God

10:1-27 – The leaders who sealed the covenant

In 9:38 we were told that the people had determined to make a written covenant with God. This was to be sealed by the leaders (princes), Levites, and priests. In this chapter we are told who sealed it and what the covenant contained.

First, verses 1-27 list the names of those who sealed the covenant. The list includes Nehemiah the governor (verse 1) followed by specific priests (verses 1-8), then Levites (verses 9-13), and then the leaders or princes (verses 14-26).

To "seal" a covenant was to officially ratify it. It may be compared to signing ones name to a contract today. In fact, these men may have physically signed this covenant, but in any case they by some means agreed to have their names attached to the terms of the covenant.

Note how this commits a person to a matter. This was not just a minor promise made by these people. They signed their names to a written covenant. The New Testament does not require such a signature, but one who commits himself must seal his covenant commitment by baptism (compare Romans 6).

10:28,29 – The other people joined in the covenant

The rest of the people did not apparently actually sign the covenant, but they still committed themselves to abide by its terms. This included the people, the priests, and the Levites (presumably the "rest" of these groups other than those who signed it).

Also included were the gatekeepers and singers – see on Nehemiah 7:1. Also mentioned were the Nethinim. These were temple servants who had been appointed by David to help the Levites in their work (see on Ezra 8:20; 2:43-58).

All these people committed themselves to separate from the people of the land to do God's law (compare 9:2). Also included were their wives, sons, and daughters, all who had knowledge and understanding. This would include all who were capable of accepting the responsibility for making the commitment to keep the covenant and obey the commands (verse 29).

Note the similarity here to the New Testament concept of "age of accountability." In the New Testament, before accepting the commitment of covenant relationship with God, sons and daughters must be old enough to know and understand the commitment they are making and to make it by their own free choice. See Mark 16:15,16; John 6:44,45; Acts 2:36,41; Galatians 3:26,27; Acts 8:12; 2:38; Romans 10:9,10; Acts 8:35-39.

The commitment to obey God

Verse 29 describes in general terms what the people were committing themselves to do. They entered into a curse and an oath to obey God's Law, given by Moses, and to observe all the commandments and ordinances of the Lord (2 Kings 23:3; 2 Chronicles 34:31). In chapter 9 the people had confessed at great length their past failure to keep God's law despite all His goodness to them. Having repented and confessed these sins, the people here made a solemn covenant to keep God's law in the future.

This involved an oath (solemn vow or promise) to keep the covenant along with a curse – a statement acknowledging the penalty upon them if they disobeyed. See Deuteronomy 29:12; Nehemiah 5:12; Psalm 119:106.

Again, while the New Testament does not require a vow as such, when we become Christians we are making just as solemn a commitment to obey God. In fact, such a commitment is the essence of conversion and of spiritual restoration from sin. One who has not been serving God must recognize his error, commit himself to turn from error (repentance), confess it, and then begin to practice what is right. This is what these people did.

All this resulted from their study of God's word (chapter 8,9) and their recognition of God's goodness and their own sins. Note they were committing themselves to follow God's laws, written 1000 years or so earlier by Moses. This written word (Scripture) still had power to guide them, and they still had power to understand it.

People sometimes today claim we cannot understand the Bible or it has no effect today, since we live 2000 years after it was written. Or they claim we cannot restore God's service today since people have been in error for long periods of time, etc. But all the reasons why restoration will not work today would have applied in Nehemiah's day. And all the reasons why it did work then are reasons why we can be sure it will work today. All we must do is study God's word, turn from sin, and commit ourselves to truly obey.

10:30,31 – Specifics of the covenant

Having committed themselves to obey God's law in general, the people then specified certain requirements of the law that they intended to keep. These presumably involved matters that they had not been properly observing.

Note that we today must likewise realize that we cannot please God simply by professing a general adherence to God's law. We must follow through with observing specific laws given by God, else our general commitment is meaningless.

Separation from surrounding nations

They committed themselves not to intermarry with people of the land. They would not give their daughters as wives to the people of the land, nor would they take the daughters of the land to marry their sons. The law expressly forbade such marriages, because the people of God would be influenced to participate in idolatry and other sins common among the inhabitants of the land. Yet such intermarriage was a common problem among the returned captives. See notes on Ezra 9,10; compare Exodus 34:12-16; Deuteronomy 7:1-3.

Observance of the holy days, including the Sabbath

The people also agreed that they would not do business on the Sabbath day. Specifically, they would not buy and sell wares with the people of the land on the Sabbath or any other holy day. God had commanded Israel to rest on the Sabbath, and specifically not to do business on that day. Many other holy days also involved days of rest. The people agreed to observe these laws. See Exodus 20:8; 34:21; 31:12-17; Leviticus 23:3,8; Deuteronomy 5:12; Jeremiah 17:27.

Note that the Sabbath law was associated with the holy days, as it is so often done in the Old Testament (see verse 33), and with laws of the seventh-year rest and release of debts. If the other holy days and other laws are not binding under the New Testament, why should we think the Sabbath is still binding? See Colossians 2:13-17; Hebrews 10:1-10; 7:11-14; 8:6-13; 9:1-4; 2 Corinthians 3:6-11; Galatians 3:24,25; 5:1-6; Romans 7:1-7; Ephesians 2:11-16.

For further information, see our articles about the Sabbath and the old law at our Bible Instruction web site at www.gospelway.com/instruct/.

Observance of the seventh-year Sabbath and release

They also determined to "forego the seventh year's produce" and the exacting of debts. This refers to the fact that the law required every seventh year the land would not be planted but would be allowed to rest – Exodus 23:10,11; Leviticus 25:4. Also on the seventh year all Israelite slaves were to be released – Jeremiah 34:14 (see discussion on Nehemiah 5). Also there was a release of debts on the seventh year (Deuteronomy 15:1-6). On the year of jubilee every fifty years all property was returned. But the seventh-year release appears to be something different. Perhaps in that year people did not have to make payments on their debts, since they would have so much less income as a result of not planting and harvesting their crops. The people covenanted to observe these laws.

10:32,33 – *Payment for the service in the temple*

The people then made ordinances for themselves to arrange to provide funds needed to do the work in the temple. This involved providing for the showbread, the regular burnt offerings on the Sabbath and the holy days, etc., and for all the work in the temple. To provide for this they determined to give 1/3 shekel per year (per person).

In Exodus 30:11-16; 38:25,26 the people had given ½ shekel in Moses' day for the tabernacle service. However, this does not appear to have been a yearly or annual payment (but note 2 Chronicles 24:6,9). But here in Nehemiah the people apparently determined to make an annual payment. This appears to be a voluntary decision of the people to support the work in the tabernacle, not required by the law itself, but determined by the people as part of their covenant (like the arrangements for the wood in verse 34). On the other hand, if the tax in Moses' day was an annual requirement, they people were here just agreeing to abide by it, as with the other laws in the list. But in that case, I don't understand the slight difference in the amount of the tax. See Matthew 17:24ff.

10:34 – *Wood for temple service*

Another need for the temple service was wood to burn on the altar in the sacrifices (Leviticus 6:12). This need was met by determining to cast lots among the priests, the Levites, and the people to take turns from time to time to bring in wood as needed. See also Nehemiah 13:31. Again, this was decided as part of the covenant of the people with God.

10:35-39 – *The firstfruits and the firstborn and the tithes*

The people also agreed to obey the laws of God regarding giving Him the firstfruits of the harvest and the firstborn of the people and animals.

Every year the people were required to give to God the firstfruits of the harvest from the ground, the trees and vineyards, etc. This was to be given to support the priests. See the commands in Exodus 23:19; 34:26; Numbers 18:12; Deuteronomy 18:4; 26:1,2. The reference to the dough in verse 37 perhaps refers to the fact that sometimes the firstfruits of the grain was ground to flour and used to make dough for bread, then it was offered as part of a heave offering. See also Numbers 15:19.

The firstborn children and firstborn animals were also to be given to God's service. This was taught in Exodus 22:29f as a consequence of the fact God spared the firstborn of Israel when He slew the firstborn Egyptians to persuade Egypt to allow Israel to go free. From then on God claimed the firstborn as His. Later, however, He accepted the tribe of Levi as His special servants in exchange for the firstborn human sons, but still the people had to bring a special sacrifice and pay a redemption fee at the birth of a firstborn. See Numbers 3:12-51; 18:13-20. The firstborn animals were to be sacrificed to God unless they were not suitable for sacrifices, in which case a redemption fee was paid. The reference here must be that the people agreed to bring the firstborn sons and animals to the temple to give the offerings and pay the redemption fees. See Exodus 13:11-15; Leviticus 27:26,27. Note also Luke 2:22-24 regarding the sacrifice offered at Jesus' birth.

They also agreed to bring to the Lord the heave offerings the law required and to pay the tithes. The tithes were one tenth of their income, which was to be paid for the support of the Levites (Leviticus 27:30-33; Numbers 18:21-32; Malachi 3:10.

The people agreed to bring all these to the temple to be placed there in the storerooms till needed.

Numbers 18:26 showed that, when the Levites received the tithes from the people, they were in turn to give a tithe (tenth) of that to support the priests in the temple. So here in Nehemiah the Levites agreed to do this, bringing it to the temple to be placed in the storerooms. This was done under the supervision of the high priest descended from Aaron.

Also the other offerings of the people, whether grain, wine, or oil, would be brought to the storerooms and kept there for use in the temple service. This is where the priests, gatekeepers, and singers were. All this was to insure that the service to God in the temple was not neglected. Deuteronomy 12:6,11; 1 Chronicles 9:26; 2 Chronicles 31:11,12; Nehemiah 13:12.

Nehemiah Chapter 11

The People Who Dwelt in the City – Chapter 11

11:1,2 – *Jerusalem needed one out of every ten people to dwell in it.*

Since Jerusalem's walls had been rebuilt, it was necessary for a sufficient number of people to inhabit the city. Perhaps this included people to defend the city, carry on business, etc.

The leaders of the people already dwelt in the city, as you might expect for the capital city. But it was decided that they needed one tenth of other people in the city, so they cast lots to decide which people would live there. The other nine tenths were to dwell in the other cities of the land. For more information about casting lots see Nehemiah 10:34; 11:1; Acts 1:24-26; Leviticus 16:8; Joshua 14:2; 1 Samuel 14:41,42; Proverbs 16:33 (Psalms 22:18).

Since this required many people to make sacrifices (such as moving and perhaps leaving ones inherited possession in the land – compare verse 3), the people who were willing to live in Jerusalem were blessed and appreciated by the other people. (I wonder if the reference to "willingly offered" means that some people simply volunteered to go. If so, did this reduce the need for others to go as a result of the lots?)

11:3-6 – *People of Judah who lived in Jerusalem*

Many people of various kinds lived in other cities according to their inheritance, but the following verses then list the chief people who lived in Jerusalem. Many were of descendants of Judah, others were of the tribe of Benjamin.

Verses 4-6 specifically lists leaders of the tribe of Judah who lived in Jerusalem. A total of four hundred sixty-eight valiant men lived there (one wonders if this counted only those who were of military age, since that was done in other censuses).

11:7-9 – *People of Benjamin who lived in Jerusalem*

These verses then list leaders of the people of the tribe of Benjamin who lived in Jerusalem. The total men of the tribe of Benjamin was nine hundred twenty-eight. Joel oversaw the people in the city, having Judah as his second in command.

11:10-14 – *Priests who lived in Jerusalem*

These verses list leaders of the priests who lived in Jerusalem. Eight hundred twenty-two did the work of the house of God. Two hundred forty-two are called heads of fathers' houses. And one hundred twenty-eight are called mighty men of valor. However, I am not sure exactly what the distinction was between these different groups.

The priests, of course, had to be descendants of Aaron, and they led in the worship in the temple (verse 11).

11:15-18 – *Levites who lived in Jerusalem*

These verses then list the leaders of the Levites who lived in Jerusalem. These had oversight of the business outside the temple (verse 16). Remember that Levites could not serve inside the temple and could not touch the holy articles. So they served outside.

In addition Mattaniah is named (verse 17) as leading the thanksgiving in prayer. The total Levites were two hundred eighty-four.

11:19-21 – *Other groups*

The gatekeepers or porters guarded the gates of the city. There were one hundred seventy-two of them.

The rest of the people lived in their various family inheritances throughout the land. This included other priests and Levites.

Also the Nethinim lived in a place named Ophel. The Nethinim were people who assisted the Levites in their jobs around the temple. See Ezra 8:20.

11:22,23 – *The singers*

The overseer of the Levites at Jerusalem was a man named Uzzi. He was also a descendant of Asaph, so he was one of the singers in charge of the worship in the temple.

Further information is given telling that the king had commanded a daily income to be appointed for the singers who led the worship in the temple.

11:24 – *The king's deputy*

Verse 24 states that the deputy of the king was a man named Pethahiah of the tribe of Judah. He apparently represented the Persian king in all matters concerning the people. Though the Israelites had been allowed to return to Judah, the king of Persia still maintained power over them. This man was apparently his appointed representative.

11:25-36 – People living in the other cities of Judah

These verses simply list other cities where various Jews lived. Verses 25-30 list cities were people of Judah lived. They generally lived south of Jerusalem (verse 30). Verses 31-36 list verses where people of Benjamin lived.

We are also told that some of the Levites that had been assigned to Judea lived in the territory of Benjamin.

Nehemiah Chapter 12

The Dedication of the Wall – Chapter 12

A Genealogy of the Priests and Levites

12:1-7 – List of the priests who returned with Zerubbabel

Verses 1-26 names the priests and Levites who had returned with Zerubbabel in the first group, along with some of their descendants. Perhaps these lists are included because the priests and Levites led in the celebration of the wall in the last part of this chapter.

Verses 1-7 lists the heads of the priests in the days of Jeshua, who came up with Zerubbabel. Ezra 2 and Nehemiah 7:6ff had listed some of the people in general who returned with Zerubbabel. These verses lists the leaders of the priests in that group.

12:8-11 – The Levites who came with Zerubbabel and Jeshua

The priests were of the tribe of Levi, but the other Levites were assigned to help the priests in their work in the temple. These verses list Levites with Jeshua, the high priest who had come with Zerubbabel.

It includes those who led in the praises and thanksgiving to God (verse 8). It also lists the descendants of Jeshua, who would also have served as priests, perhaps as high priests.

12:12-21 – Priests who were in the days of Jeshua's son Joiakim

Verse 10 says that Jeshua's son was Joiakim. These verses list the priests who served in the days of Joiakim. These appear to be the sons of the priests listed in verses 1-7.

12:22,23 – Priests during the days of Joiakim's son Eliashib and his sons

Verses 10,11 listed the descendants of Jeshua, including his son Joiakim and Joiakim's son Eliashib, etc. This verse simply informs us that a record of the heads of the houses of the priests and Levites were kept during the reign of Darius the Persian in the days of these descendants of Jeshua till Jaddua.

And heads of the houses of the Levites till Eliashib's descendant Johana were written in the book of the chronicles. (I am not sure what chronicles this refers to. I cannot find this information in the Old Testament books of 1 or 2 Chronicles. But the reference here could be to some other chronicles, which may not have been important enough to place in the inspired record.)

12:24-26 – List of the Levites of the next generation

Verses 8,9 had listed leaders of the Levites during the days of Jeshua, including those who led in thanksgiving. Now these verses list leading men among the Levites who lived during the days of Joiakim, son of Jeshua the priest. These would have been descendants of the Levites named in verses 8,9 and would have lived during the days of Nehemiah the governor and Ezra the priest and scribe.

Again he lists those who led in giving thanks. These were organized in the manner arranged by David. Also listed are those who were gatekeepers or porters. These would guard the storerooms (presumably where the gifts described in 10:35-39 were kept).

Dedication of the Wall

12:27-29 – Levites came to Jerusalem for the dedication of the wall.

Nehemiah here returns to the discussion of the wall. He describes the celebration that occurred when the wall was dedicated after its completion. Since this was to be a big celebration, the Levites were brought into Jerusalem to lead it. They lived in other villages around Jerusalem (verses 28,29).

The Levites were to lead the thanksgiving and singing at the dedication, also using various instruments of music. Most likely the songs used were religious and involved praise to God. But we remember that the Old Testament expressly allowed for the use of instrumental music in such worship. See 1 Chronicles 25:6; 2 Chronicles 5:13; 7:6. Once again, the contrast to the New Testament, rather than convincing us to use instruments in worship today, shows that God has not approved such for today. When they were allowed in the Old Testament, they were clearly and expressly named and described. If God wants them today, why are they not likewise today named and described?

For further information, see our articles about instrumental music in worship at our Bible Instruction web site at **www.gospelway.com/instruct/**.

12:30 – The priests and Levites purified themselves, the people, the gates, and the wall.

In preparation for the dedication ceremony, the priests and Levites performed ceremonial purifications for themselves, the people, the gates, and the wall. No one could participate in any congregational worship if he was ceremonially unclean, and no one could touch what was unclean without himself becoming unclean. The laws of cleanness and uncleanness related to such things as touching a dead body, secretion of various body fluids, etc. Before these leaders could purify others, they first had to purify themselves.

See Ezra 6:20; Nehemiah 13:22,30.

12:31-37 – The first group of celebrants described

The celebration consisted of two large groups of choirs or singers who marched around the wall in opposite directions. They apparently both began at one point of the wall, then one group marched in one direction around the wall, while the other group marched in the other direction. Then they met on the other side of the city. As they went, they praised God and gave thanks.

The first group is here described. It was led by Ezra the scribe (verse 36). From the original meeting place, this group traveled to the right toward the Refuse or Dung gate. Various leaders who went with them are named, and some of the points they passed on the wall are named. Apparently the wall had stairs at one point, at least, that this group had to ascend.

12:38,39 – The second group described

Nehemiah accompanied the second group that marched the opposite direction around the wall. These verses describe some of the gates and towers on the wall that they passed. They too offered thanksgiving as they marched.

12:40-43 – The two groups met at the temple to worship.

The two groups of worshipers then met and worshiped at the temple, the house of God. These verses then name some of the leaders of the group that accompanied Nehemiah. Some played trumpets, and others sang led by a director.

Having met at the temple, they then offered sacrifices to God and rejoiced. Apparently those who marched around the walls were men, but the women and children met them at the temple and joined them in rejoicing and praising God, so that the sound of the rejoicing could be heard afar off.

In this way the wall was dedicated, and the people expressed their joy in having completed it. The reason for their joy was attributed to God for His blessings to them.

12:44 – *People appointed various remaining jobs*

Besides the dedication of the wall, the people took the opportunity to appoint other tasks to various people. In particular, some were put in charge of the rooms where the gifts of the people would be stored. These included the offerings, firstfruits, tithes, etc., as required by the law. In chapter 10, as part of their covenant to serve God, the people had promised to bring in these gifts to the temple. The people of Judah likewise rejoiced for the ministry of the priests and Levites.

12:45-47 – *Portions set aside for the singers and gatekeepers*

The priests and Levites performed the duties that had been assigned to them. But the singers and the gatekeepers had been organized and assigned duties by David and Solomon. In particular, the singers had been led by Asaph. They led the people in praising and thanking God. See 1 Chronicles 25 & 26; 2 Chronicles 29:30.

In the days of Zerubbabel and in the days of Nehemiah, portions were given to provide for these singers and for the gatekeepers. They were given a portion for their provision each day. So the Levites and priests and all the spiritual leaders were provided for by the people. See notes on chapter 10; compare Numbers 18:21,24.

Nehemiah Chapter 13

Spiritual Renewal of the People – Chapter 13

Step #12 in Useful Service to God: Remind People of Their Commitment to God and Rebuke Disobedience

In Nehemiah 10 the people had renewed their commitment to keep God's law. They had even made a specific covenant to do so. In this chapter Nehemiah tells how the people failed in many ways to keep that covenant, so he had to remind them and insist that they keep the covenant and continue serving God.

13:1-3 – Moabites and Ammonites were separated from the people.

On a certain day (what day I cannot tell), the people read in the Book of Moses that no Ammonite or Moabite could come into the assembly of the people of God. This is recorded in Deuteronomy 23:3-6. The reason given was that these nations had not welcomed the Israelites (with bread and water) when they came to Canaan after leaving Egyptian slavery. Instead, they had hired Balaam to curse Israel (as recorded in Numbers 22,23).

These nations were descendants of Abraham's nephew Lot, so they were related to the Israelites. They should have been hospitable and kind to Israel. Instead, they had sought to harm them, even seeking to turn God against them. It did not work, because God turned the curse into a blessing, and eventually Israel captured Canaan despite the opposition of these nations. But God pronounced a curse on them (instead of their curse on Israel), saying they could never enter the assembly of Israel. Apparently this forbade, allowing such people to come into any religious assembly of the nation. Verses 23ff make clear that the people were also forbidden to intermarry with such people.

By reading the law, the people were able to understand this restriction and use it to restore their proper conduct before God. Once again, as earlier discussed, restoration is possible when people will read and obey the law. Though the law had been written many centuries before and had been extensively disobeyed and ignored, yet the people could understand it, obey it, and thereby restore their relationship to God.

The Jews in Nehemiah's day had become lax regarding this law. On reading the law, however, they determined to obey it, so they separated themselves from these forbidden people. Similar language was used in 9:2 and 10:28, where they separated themselves from the people of the land (these were not necessarily Moabites and Ammonites). Note that the people not only committed sin, but they had problems staying right when they repented. In a few years they would again disobey the same laws.

Disobedience to God's law was bad, but the willingness to repent and obey was praiseworthy. Again, when people have hearts willing to obey God, study of His word reveals how we ought to live.

13:4,5 – *Eliashib, who was allied with Tobiah, gave him a room as part of the temple grounds.*

Verse 6 tells us that Nehemiah had been absent from Jerusalem for a time. During this time the people fell into various sins. When he returned, he had to lead the people to repent and keep their covenant regarding God's service.

One problem that reappeared during this time related to one of the old enemies of Nehemiah, namely Tobiah. This Tobiah was an Ammonite, one of the very kind of people that we just read should be put out from the assemblies of God's people. Instead, he was one of the people that the Jews had not separated from as they should have separated. And not only was he an Ammonite, but he had been an enemy who opposed Nehemiah's efforts to rebuild the wall, even threatening to do violence against the workers. See on 2:10,19 for other references.

Not only had the people failed to separate from him, but in fact he was an ally of the high priest Eliashib, grandson of Jeshua (compare 3:1; 12:10). In 6:17-19 we were told that he had allies among God's people who worked to get Nehemiah to accept him. Now we learn how influential these allies were.

Note how strong the influence of evil people can be, and how hard it is to remove that influence when those people have close ties with God's people, especially people in influential places. This is exactly why God had forbidden intermarriage with people of the lands. Such relationships give people influence that continually caused trouble for God's people.

Christians also need to learn this lesson. Evil companions still corrupt good morals (1 Cor. 15:33). We must have the courage to rebuke and stand against such relationships.

Note also how old enemies have a way of coming back to haunt God's people. They may be defeated once or twice, but they have a way of resurfacing to create problems.

Perversion of the temple storerooms

As high priest, Eliashib was in charge of the storerooms of the temple, the rooms that should have been used to store the meal offerings, vessels, tithes, and other items for support of the priests, Levites, gatekeepers, and singers. These chambers had been built for a specific legitimate purpose relating to the service in the temple. The people had specifically determined, just in 12:44, to use these storerooms for these purposes.

However, Eliashib had taken one of the large storerooms and had allowed Tobiah to use it for his personal purposes. Verse 8 shows that he had put his personal household possessions there. This perverted the purpose of the temple and hindered it from being used for the proper purpose. It also put the people in association with an Ammonite whom God said should have no part in Israel's assemblies.

Note how similar this is to many perversions today among God's people. Local churches today also purchase "chambers" (church buildings) for legitimate purposes of the church: assembling to worship God and study and teach His word. However, many churches today take those chambers and allow them to be used for activities that are no part of the church's work: parties, recreation, entertainment, and social meals. All such activities are perversions of the authorized work of local churches, just as the misuse of the temple storerooms described here.

13:6-9 – Cleansing the temple storerooms

Here Nehemiah explained that he was not in Jerusalem when these errors occurred regarding Tobiah. In the thirty-second year of Artaxerxes (12 years after he had gone to Jerusalem to build the wall – 2:1), he had returned to spend time with the king. This is apparently what the king had expected when Nehemiah went to Jerusalem – 2:6. Then after a time (how long we are not told) he left again for Jerusalem. On returning, he discovered the evil done by Eliashib and Tobiah in the house of God. Note that he clearly identifies this conduct as "evil."

Note that evil people may be defeated in their cause. But when the leaders are gone, who had firmly opposed them, the enemies may attempt again to assert themselves and regain power without repenting. God's people must be on guard to continually oppose error.

Nehemiah grieved when he learned of the error. Again we are shown the great concern he had for the people. He was touched when their conduct or circumstances were harmful to them. This ought to be how we feel when we see others, especially God's people in sin or suffering.

He then took firm action and solved the problem by simply casting Tobiah's household stuff out of the temple chamber. This was easy enough to do of itself. However, Nehemiah had the advantage of having authority to do it without others harming him for so doing. He did not take the law into his own hands, but rather he administered the law as was his duty to do. Likewise today, those who pervert the purpose of the church must be disciplined if they will not repent.

He then commanded that the temple be cleansed and the rooms returned to their proper purpose for storing the grain offering and other supplies for those who served in the temple.

Note that, not only was Tobiah using a part of the temple grounds for that for which it should not have been used, but also in so doing he was hindering or preventing its use for its proper purpose. As long as the storeroom contained Tobiah's property, it could not be used to store the supplies for the temple workers as it should have been used. The error was both in using it for an unauthorized purpose and hindering its use for authorized work.

This is exactly the same for the unauthorized activities that people often today bring into the work of the church. Such activities as entertainment, recreation, parties, and social meals, when they are brought into the work of the church, inevitably they eventually push out the spiritual work that the church ought to be doing. The church and its members have limits on their time, money, and energy. When the church becomes involved in unauthorized activities with physical and carnal emphasis, like those mentioned, the result will be to limit or hinder the church's involvement in the authorized spiritual activities of worship, teaching, Bible study, and saving the lost.

These physical or secular activities may not be wrong for individuals to practice, but the church should not waste its resources and facilities on them. When they are introduced into the church activities, they will inevitably progress to more and more secular involvement, pushing out spirituality. The result is denominations today that are so wrapped up in material pursuits that they are nothing more than social clubs and general welfare societies. But it all begins with perversion of church work into some unauthorized secular activity, just as in this story in Nehemiah. We must oppose it from the beginning if we seek to prevent the proliferation of error.

Note the similarity to Jesus who likewise cast out the moneychangers and those who bought and sold from the temple. The problem and the solution were similar to Nehemiah's case. The people had perverted the temple from its authorized spiritual purpose. The solution was to remove the unauthorized activity.

Note the courage that Nehemiah showed in opposing the error. Surely other people had seen that this activity was a violation of the covenant and purpose of the people in chapter 10 and 12, yet so far no one had done anything. We too need the courage to cast out unauthorized activities from Jesus' church. God's faithful servants simply must not stand idly by and allow God's spiritual creations, built for the sake of spiritual purposes, to be perverted for secular and material purposes. We must speak out. And if people will not recognize the error and repent, then we must have the courage to exercise authorized discipline to remove them.

For further information, see our article about church organization and work at our Bible Instruction web site at www.gospelway.com/instruct/.

Note that Artaxerxes is called king of Babylon in verse 6. See Ezra 5:13 where Cyrus was also called king of Babylon. Although these were kings of Persia, evidently they are for some reason also called kings of Babylon. Perhaps it is because they took over the empire from Babylon. Or perhaps they had for a time actually ruled the region of Babylon in their upward ascendancy to power over the whole empire. For whatever, the reason, the language is apparently not a falsehood.

13:10,11 – The temple servants had also not been properly supported.

The next problem Nehemiah observed was that the Levites and singers (and presumably other temple workers) had not been provided the support (portions) that the law required they be given. This duty to provide for the Levites was part of the covenant that the people had expressly agreed to accomplish in 10:32-39. Here we are just a few years later and they are failing to keep the law of God and to keep the covenant they had so energetically made. Note how easily God's people may become discouraged and begin to neglect the work they commit themselves to do.

Since the temple workers had no support, they had gone back to working in their fields. No doubt they were discouraged, but they also had to have some kind of support. So they had to leave the temple work to obtain income for themselves and their families.

So Nehemiah confronted the rulers of the Jews about this and asked why God's house was forsaken. He then gathered them together and set them again in their place. I can only conclude that this must refer to the workers in the temple who had gone to their fields. He brought them back to the temple to put them in their assigned duties.

All of this also was surely related to Tobiah's use of the storeroom. When the rooms were used for his personal property, they were not available to store the portions to support the temple workers. The two go hand-in-hand: changing the direction of God's work from spiritual activity to material pursuits leads God's people both to involve themselves in things they should not be doing and to neglect things they should be doing.

This is further evidence of the danger of the church today getting involved in unauthorized secular activities. As resources are diverted to these physical pursuits, less and less time, resources, facilities, and effort will be directed toward the authorized spiritual work.

13:12-14 – Support for the temple workers was restored.

When Nehemiah urged the leaders to return to providing for the temple workers and had cleansed the storerooms and arranged for the workers to return, the people again brought in the provisions to the storehouse. Nehemiah then appointed men to serve as treasurers to be in charge of these provisions to see that they were distributed properly.

Verse 13 names the men appointed and affirms that they were faithful men who would do their work properly. Men appointed to responsible positions among God's people must be trustworthy. In this case there was possibility for theft or misuse of these provisions, so reliable, honest men were needed.

Nehemiah then prayed to God to remember what he had done for the good of the service in the temple. He calls on God to not wipe out or forget what he had done. Of course, God never forgets our good deeds, but Nehemiah is simply calling on God to keep His promises in this matter.

13:15-18 – Nehemiah rebuked the people for violating the Sabbath.

Another error committed by the people then came to Nehemiah's attention. People were violating the Sabbath by working for gain on the seventh day. Such work was expressly forbidden - see Exodus 20:8-11; 31:12-17; etc.

Yet people among the Jews were treading winepresses on the Sabbath, bringing in sheaves of grain, putting them on their donkeys, and carrying various produce and other burdens into Jerusalem and selling them on the Sabbath. Nehemiah warned them about this violation of the seventh day of the week.

Some of the men involved were foreign traders from Tyre, who brought fish and other goods to sell to the inhabitants of Jerusalem on the Sabbath. All this violated, not just the Sabbath law, but also the covenant the people had expressly made in 10:31.

So once again Nehemiah had to contend with the rulers of the people and call them into account for another sin, this time for violation of the Sabbath. He reminded them that sins like this were what had caused God to send the people into captivity. The people knew about this. They had just a few years earlier rebuilt the wall that had been destroyed when they went into captivity. Yet they were repeating the same kinds of errors (compare Jer. 17:21-27).

How different are people today? We do not have a specific Sabbath command not to work on a certain day of the week, but we do have commands to assemble to worship God. Yet how many people simply choose to pursue material interests when they could arrange to be worshiping God? Many will accept voluntary overtime, keep their businesses open, or schedule themselves to work during church meetings, when they could rearrange their work schedules to attend church meetings. Do they make an effort to trade shifts, avoid voluntary overtime if it conflicts, or even change jobs if necessary to avoid frequently missing?

Others choose to attend sports, entertainment, recreation, or musical functions instead of worshiping God and studying His word? How does this differ in principle from those here in Nehemiah who, for their own personal profit, neglected the spiritual service of God? We should be willing to suffer financial loss, if necessary, in order to obey God's commands and worship Him. See Matthew 6:19-33; 16:24-27; Romans 8:5-8; 12:1,2; 2 Corinthians 8:5; 10:3,4; John 6:27,63; Luke 12:15-21; 1 Timothy 6:6-10; Colossians 3:1,2.

13:19-22 – Nehemiah promoted Sabbath observance.

Nehemiah took steps to prevent people from doing business on the Sabbath. He had already talked to the leaders. Further, he had the gates of the city closed as the Sabbath began when the day grew dark (days were measured from sundown to sundown). The gates could not be opened again till the Sabbath was over. This would keep people from coming into the city to sell on the Sabbath. He also sent some servants to guard the gates to make sure no burdens were carried in or out on the Sabbath. Compare Jeremiah 17:21,22.

This kept people from carrying burdens in on the Sabbath; but then the traders simply made camp outside the city gates, waiting to come in as soon as the gates were opened. Nehemiah would not have this either, but rebuked them and warned them that, if they stayed, he would lay hands on them (arrest them). The result was that they altogether ceased to come on the Sabbath.

He then commanded the Levites to accept the responsibility to guard the gates to make sure that the Sabbath was kept holy and not violated. He then called on God once again to remember the good that he had done and to show mercy and goodness to Nehemiah to spare him (compare verse 14).

13:23,24 – Jews it also intermarried with people of the land.

Verses 1-3 had discussed failure of the Jews to separate themselves from the Ammonites and Moabites. Now Nehemiah begins to discuss a related problem in which the people were intermarrying with people of the land, Ashdod, Ammon, and Moab. Not only were they allowing them into the assembly, they were actually marrying them.

The people had a similar problem just twenty-five or so years earlier. As soon as Ezra had brought his group back from captivity, he discovered much intermarriage between Jews and people of the surrounding nations. He had led them to give up their wives on that occasion. See notes on Ezra 9 and 10 regarding this problem and the Scriptures it violated. (However, remember that Ruth was a Moabitess, whom God allowed to marry Boaz and even included her in Jesus' ancestry. There must have been some exceptions, such as genuine conversion as a proselyte.)

As a result of this intermarriage, half the children could not speak the Jew's language (presumably did not speak it clearly or well), but spoke the language of the foreign parent. This illustrates one of the more tragic problem areas caused by such intermarriages: the effects on the children. Not only did intermarriage endanger the servant of God to become unfaithful, but it subjected the children to ungodly influences that may cause them to be lost.

Children will be influenced by both parents, as illustrated here by the speech of these children. But godly parents should raise their children to serve the true God (Proverbs 22:6; Ephesians 6:4). The harmful spiritual influence of the ungodly parent is reason enough to avoid such marriage. Even if the servant of God remains faithful and does not fall away, chances are very slim that all the children will grow up to be faithful. Almost invariably one or more is lost. It is bad enough that parents choose to endanger their own souls, but their children have no choice who their parents will be. Intermarriage causes the children to be born into an influence that puts their souls at eternal risk without their choice or knowledge in the matter.

This example also shows the influence of people on others and the danger of compromising with sin in general. Just as these foreign parents influenced their children, so we are often influenced by people even if they are not our parents or family members. We want to have our cake and eat it too. We want to try to serve God yet maintain close ties to sinners or tempting people, places, and activities.

Such associations frequently lead Christians into sin. See Proverbs 4:23; 6:27; 13:20; 22:3; Matthew 5:8; 6:13; 18:8,9; Romans 13:14; 1 Corinthians 15:33; Genesis 39:7-12. If this can be true just of friendships, how much more so can ungodly spouse or parents influence people for harm? This is why God expressly forbade such marriages in the Old Testament and why they are foolish and dangerous still today.

13:25-28 – Nehemiah required separation, reminding the people Solomon sinned because of intermarriage.

Again Nehemiah contended with the people for their sins. They were violating God's law (see on Ezra 9,10). But they were also violating the covenant vow they had made to God just a few years earlier in

10:29. They had then expressly vowed to God that they would not do this kind of thing.

So Nehemiah pronounced curses upon them, beat some of them, and plucked out their hair (all of these were valid punishments under the Old Testament law). Then he made them once again take a vow (as in their former covenant) not to allow intermarriage with people of the land.

He also reminded the people of past examples of those who committed this error. Specifically, Solomon, though he had been highly blessed of God as king of Israel and the son of godly David, yet he was led into sin by his foreign wives (compare 1 Kings 11:1ff). They had influenced him to commit all kinds of idolatry. Surely people in Nehemiah's day and likewise today are foolish to think they can avoid the temptation that even the wise man Solomon succumbed to. If we marry people who do not serve God, what makes us think we will not go astray like he did? Nehemiah then asked the people why they were transgressing God's law by marrying such people.

Next a specific instance is given. We are told that a son of Joiada, who was in turn a son of Eliashib the high priest, had married the daughter of Sanballat, who was a Horonite! Sanballat, of course, was another of the enemies who had attempted to stop Nehemiah and the people from rebuilding the wall, even threatening violence against them (see notes regarding Tobiah on verses 4-8 above). Not only was the high priest Eliashib himself allied with the enemy Tobiah, but Eliashib's grandson was married to a daughter of the enemy Sanballat. This was an express violation of God's law against intermarrying foreign wives and an express violation of the covenant of the people in chapter 10.

This example shows the powerful influence that can be caused by fraternizing with the enemy. When God's people form close associations with people in sin, the result harms other people of God. And the problem is magnified when those who are guilty are leaders. In this case, both the alliance with Tobiah and the alliance with Sanballat led the high priest and his family into sin.

Nehemiah dealt with this by chasing Sanballat's son-in-law from his presence. This clearly implies that he was removed from among the people of God, which was the proper discipline for people who committed such sin but would not repent. This passage does not mention that those who intermarried had to give up those wives, but this example shows that those who did not do so were driven from among the people. This also shows that people today who live in unscriptural remarriages, which today are an express violation of God's law, should likewise be disciplined by withdrawal if they will not repent. Such discipline is needed both to motivate the sinner to repent and to remove the sinful influence from among God's people.

13:29-31 – Nehemiah asked God to remember him for the good he had done.

Just as Nehemiah had called on God to remember his righteous deeds, so he here called on God to remember those who had sinned and defiled the priesthood and the covenant of priests and Levites. Such intermarriage was a sin for any Israelite, but especially for a priest. God, of course, will remember both good and bad of all that we do.

He then summarizes that he had cleansed them of everything pagan or heathen. This appears to especially refer to the priests and Levites. Note that all pagan religious practices and influences must be removed from the worship God's people offer to God. He then appointed the purified priests and Levites to their duties and services. He also appointed the responsibilities to provide for their support by offerings and firstfruits.

All these works Nehemiah had done according to God's will. He then concludes by once again calling on God to remember him and bless him for good (compare verses 14,22). Surely Nehemiah was a good and godly leader. We can learn many lessons from him about useful service to God and helping God's people serve Him. Let us study diligently such godly men, learn the lessons, and apply them in our own lives that God can also remember us for good.

Introduction to the Book of Esther

Background of the Book

Theme
An historical narrative showing how God spared the people of Israel in exile by means of a courageous Jewish maiden

Author
The inspired author is unknown. Horne states:

> Concerning the author of this book, the opinions of Bible critics are so greatly divided, that it is difficult to determine by whom it was written. ... Augustine is of opinion that this book was written by Ezra; which is perhaps more probable than any that have been offered...

He further adds, "it has always been received as canonical by the Jews, who hold this book in the highest estimation..."

Location
Events occurred in Shushan (Susa) the capital of Persia during the reign of Ahasuerus (Xerxes) – 1:2. (See **map**.) Although many Jews had been permitted to return to Judea under a decree by Cyrus, many Jews remained in Persia or lands where they had been taken captive.

Main characters
Ahasuerus (Xerxes) - King of Persia
Haman – Chief of all the princes under Ahasuerus
Mordecai – A Jew in Shushan, a Benjamite, yet loyal to the king
Esther – A beautiful Jewish maiden, orphaned but raised by Mordecai, her cousin (his uncle's daughter – 2:7)

Summary of contents by section:
Chapter 1,2 — Esther becomes queen in place of Vashti
Chapter 3-5 — Haman rises to power and plots the death of Mordecai and the Jews

Chapter 4-7 —Esther pleads on behalf of her people; Haman is slain

Chapter 8-10 – Jews win the victory over their enemies

Historical Setting

Events in the book of Esther occur in Persia during the period of restoration of the Jews from Babylonian captivity. When Persia came to power after defeating Babylon, they allowed captives to return to their homelands. The story of Esther began in the third year of Xerxes (1:3), after Zerubbabel had led the first group of Jews to return under Cyrus, but before Ezra led the second group to return under Artaxerxes (see introductory notes on Ezra and Nehemiah).

Major empires of the ancient world:

* Assyria – overthrew Israel (northern tribes)
* Babylon – overthrew Judah under Nebuchadnezzar
* Medo-Persia – overthrew Babylon in 538 BC
    Cyrus – decreed return of the Jews to Judea
    Cambyses – 530-522 BC
    Darius "the Great" – 522-486 BC
    Xerxes (Ahasuerus) of the Book of Esther – 486-465 BC (NKJV footnote on 1:1 says 485-464 BC)
    Artaxerxes – 465-424 BC
    (These were followed by other minor rulers)
* Greek – Alexander the Great defeated Persia
* Roman

Esther Chapter 1

Esther Replaces Vashti as Queen – Chapter 1,2

Vashti Angers the King and He Determines to Remove Her - Chapter 1

1:1,2 – *These events occurred during the reign of Ahasuerus, king of Persia, in Shushan the citadel.*

These events occurred in the reign of Ahasuerus, king of Persia. He is also called Xerxes in secular history (NKJV footnote, compare introductory notes). He ruled over 127 provinces from India to Ethiopia. Obviously, this was a great empire, the greatest of that day, having overthrown the Babylonian Empire.

The events occurred in the capital city of the empire, which is called Shushan or Susa. Specifically, they occurred in the citadel, a fortified palace.

Joseph Free points out that archaeologists excavated the palace of Xerxes at Susa, the very palace at which Esther would have lived. He says:

> The building covered two and one-half acres, and included a beautiful throne-room which was decorated with thirty-six fluted columns, each being some sixty-seven feet high and supporting a ceiling of Lebanon cedar. The capitals of the pillars were formed of the heads and shoulders of oxen, placed back to back. ... The finds at Susa from the period of Xerxes were so astonishing that the Louvre in Paris devoted two large rooms to the exhibition of these treasures...

Holden and Geisler confirm that Xerxes and Susa are well known in history (including the location of the king's tomb) and that many details of the record of Esther agree with known archaeological facts about Persia. They explain that Xerxes was the Greek name for the king, but Ahasuerus was his name in Hebrew (pp 280,283).

1:3-5 – *The king made a feast to display his great kingdom.*

The story begins during the third year of the king's reign. The nobles, officials, and princes of the provinces he ruled were called to witness a great display demonstrating the greatness of his kingdom and majesty. The nature of this demonstration is not described exactly, but it is called a feast that lasted one hundred eighty days (six months).

At the end of these days, he had a specific feast that lasted seven days. All the people, great and small, were present in Shushan in the court of the palace garden.

1:6-8 – *The palace was decorated with beautiful furnishings.*

The palace was decorated with curtains of white and blue bound up by fine linen cords with purple on silver rods and marble pillars. People sat on couches made of silver and gold (Keil says this refers to gold and silver thread woven into the cloth of the couches), which were placed on a mosaic pavement of alabaster, turquoise, white and black marble.

The people were then given golden vessels to drink from, each vessel being different from the others. In the vessels was royal wine served in abundance. However, the law required that drinking was not compulsory. The officers of the household were instructed to provide so each person could drink as he pleased.

This describes the lavish provisions of the feast and how it demonstrates the wealth of the king and his kingdom.

According to Millard, this vast amount of gold in Susa was confirmed by the Greeks who claimed that, when Alexander the Great conquered Susa, he carried off more than a ton of gold (page 144).

1:9-12 – *Vashti refused to come before the men of the banquet.*

While the men were feasting, the queen Vashti made a feast for the women in the palace. This apparently created no problems.

However, on the seventh day of the feast, the king was merry with wine. He then commanded the seven named eunuchs to bring Vashti before the king wearing her royal crown, so the people and officials could observe her beauty. She was beautiful to behold, and the king in effect wanted to show her off.

However, Vashti refused to come despite the command of the king. This infuriated the king. This was the event that led later to the queen being deposed, as the subsequent verses show.

We may wonder at the wisdom or folly of Vashti's decision. Most commentators uphold her (especially Clarke, Keil, and Zerr). However, some question her conduct (see Henry). Whether she was justified in her refusal or not depends on exactly what the king asked her to do and what her reasons were for refusing, and this seems hard to determine.

Obviously the men at the feast were drinking and probably some were drunken. No self-respecting woman, especially if beautiful and yet modest, would want to be a toy displayed before such men. Doubtless she would be submitted to suggestive thoughts and probably even suggestive remarks. Furthermore, Oriental women were generally extremely modest, covering themselves thoroughly, especially in the presence of men. For the men to look on her beauty would require some display. She may have felt this was a violation of her dignity and/or her modesty.

On the other hand, if all she was required to display was her face, if she was not expected to expose more of herself (which some commentators suppose was expected of her), it is hard to say that she would have been wrong to go. The very fact she refused to go implies that she felt something out of the ordinary was being asked of her. It is possible, however, that she was haughty and simply determined to please herself regardless of her husband's wishes.

Perhaps we do not need to decide the right or wrong of her case, since we do not know the specifics. However, we do need to realize that God instructs women to submit to their husbands, unless they are asked to sin against God (Genesis 2:18; 3:16; Ephesians 5:22-33; Colossians 3:18; 1 Corinthians 11:3; 14:34; 1 Timothy 2:9-14; 3:4,12; Titus 2:4,5; 1 Peter 3:1-7). On the other hand, immodesty is definitely sinful, so if a husband did request his wife to practice such, she should refuse.

1:13-15 – The king consulted his advisors regarding what to do about Vashti's disobedience.

The king then called a meeting of his trusted advisors. These were wise men who understood the times. This is explained to mean that they knew the law and justice as properly applied in that society at that time (though some theorize that it might also have included the practice of Astrology). Compare 1 Chron. 12:32, which is similar and does not seem to have any reference to Astrology. The seven closest advisors are named, being the princes of Persia and Media. They had the highest rank as princes in the kingdom and so had access to the king's presence.

The king then inquired of these men what he should do about Vashti. She had disobeyed a direct command of the king taken to her by the eunuchs. He evidently thought some penalty should be assessed against her.

1:16-18 – Memucan expressed concern that Vashti's act may lead other women to disrespect their husbands.

The advisor who spoke up was Memucan (at least he is the one whose advice is recorded). He said that Vashti's conduct was not just an act of rebellion against the king, but it was a wrong done to all the princes and all the people because of its influence. The queen was so prominent that, if she were allowed to rebel against the king without consequence, then other women would follow her example and would show contempt for the authority of their husbands. The women would all hear what had happened and would use Vashti's example as justification for them to do likewise.

The principle that Memucan states here is an important principle (though we do not know that it is proper to apply it in this case). It is true that the conduct, especially of prominent people, has an influence on others. When people in positions of authority and prominence are known to practice sin, the result is harmful influence on people of the nation. This is a legitimate concern.

Of course, as discussed already, it could be that the principle is misapplied in Vashti's case. If her conduct was justified, then this is not a right conclusion in her case. In that case what could have been done would be to send a proclamation explaining to everyone why the queen did as she did. Women could still be admonished to respect their husband's authority and men would be admonished not to request their wives to act improperly.

1:19-22 – A decree was made to depose Vashti as queen.

The recommendation was that Vashti should be punished by royal decree removing her from her position as queen and forbidding her to come anymore before the king. Someone else would then be chosen as queen in her place. Such a proclamation would give all the women of the empire reason to respect the will of their husbands.

Note that we are told that, when such royal decrees were made, they were recorded in the laws of the Medo-Persian Empire and then could not be altered. No one could change them, not even the king himself. This was a fundamental law of the empire. We will see that this principle of law becomes quite significant in other applications as the story proceeds.

Such an action by the king would have the effect of a divorce, though in some technicalities it might not have actually been a divorce. She was deposed from being queen, but we will see that the king had a large harem of which only one woman would be queen. So she might still have remained in his harem. Nevertheless, she would never be favored to come before the king, so she was at least in disgrace and banished from his presence for life. Yet having been queen, it seems unlikely (to me) that she was hereby granted permission to marry some other man. If such were the case, then this was not technically a divorce. Nevertheless, if it was a divorce, such was permitted under the Old Testament law but would not be permitted under the gospel (Deut. 24:1ff; compare Matt. 19:3-9).

The king and other princes were pleased by this advice. So letters were sent to all the provinces stating the decree. These were translated into the language of each of the provinces, so that people everywhere would know that each man should be respected as head of his house.

Esther Chapter 2

Esther Is Chosen as Queen - Chapter 2

2:1 – *The king remembered Vashti's conduct.*

After some time had passed since the banishment of Vashti, King Ahasuerus thought further about her actions and the decree that had been made against her. That decree had declared that her royal estate as queen would be given to someone else (1:19), but to this date no one had been chosen as queen.

2:2-4 – *Beautiful virgins were brought so whoever pleased the king the most would become queen.*

Some of the king's servants suggested a plan. They suggested that the kingdom be canvassed for beautiful young maidens. Officers in all the provinces would seek out maidens and bring them to the palace in Shushan. There they would be placed in the house of the women – the harem such as were kept by most kings (compare Solomon).

These women were apparently to become wives and/or concubines of the king. They would be put in the keeping of a eunuch named Hegai, custodian of the women. They would then be given "beauty preparations" (compare verses 9,12) followed by an opportunity to please the king. The one who pleased him best would be chosen queen in Vashti's place. So a selection would be made from among the young maidens in the harem to find one from the group to be queen.

This plan satisfied the king, so he decreed that it be so done.

2:5,6 – *Among the captives who had been carried away from Jerusalem was a Benjamite named Mordecai.*

The record now introduces the hero and heroine of the story. Mordecai was a Jew of the tribe of Benjamin. Some of his lineage is given, and we are told that he was in Shushan the palace, though his exact responsibility there is never made clear.

Mordecai was a captive among the Jews during the days following the time in which Nebuchadnezzar, king of Babylon, had carried away as captives Jeconiah, king of Judah, and other Jews. See 2 Kings 24:6-

17; 2 Chronicles 36:10,20; Jeremiah 24:1. It is uncertain, from the reading, exactly who verse 6 refers to as having been taken captive. It could refer to Mordecai's great grandfather Kish, the last named person in the previous verse (as in the NKJV). Or it could refer to Mordecai himself (compare NKJV footnote).

Keil points out that it had been some 120 years since the beginning of the captivity. Babylon had since been overthrown by Persia, and several Persian kings had come and gone. It is unlikely that Mordecai was this old, especially if he had a cousin as young as Esther. Keil suggests that perhaps Mordecai was not born when his ancestors were carried captive, but it was still proper to speak this way since his ancestors were taken captive and he was born as their offspring in captivity.

2:7 – *Mordecai had a beautiful cousin named Esther whom he had raised because she was an orphan.*

Mordecai had a young cousin named Hadasseh (Chaldee meaning "myrtle") or Esther (Persian meaning "a star"). She was Mordecai's uncle's daughter, therefore Mordecai's cousin. But she had no living father or mother (verse 15 says her father was named Abihail). When her parents had died, Mordecai had taken her as his own daughter and raised her (see also on verse 15). She was fair and beautiful.

Lessons about caring for needy relatives

Note here an admirable quality in Mordecai. He was willing to make the effort to care for a relative in time of need. This is exactly what 1 Timothy 5 teaches Christians to do. If people today would recognize their individual responsibility to care for needy relatives, as Mordecai had done, we could solve much of the "widow and orphan" problem.

Note that Esther was a true orphan – she had neither mother nor father. Had her parents been living, they would have been responsible to care for her. But at their death she became the responsibility of a relative to individually provide for. This is God's way and is best for all involved. Today the church should care only for saints who have no relatives (in the church) to care for them. And then the church should oversee the work, rather then sending the needy person and/or a financial contribution to an institution (Acts 6; 20:28; 1 Peter 5:1-3; 1 Timothy 5).

For further information, see our article about church organization and work at our Bible Instruction web site at www.gospelway.com/instruct/.

2:8,9 – As one of the maidens who might become queen, Esther found favor with the custodian of the maidens.

When the decree was issued to bring fair maidens into the king's harem, Esther was among those chosen. Whether or not she had any choice in this selection is not stated.

She was placed under the custody of Hegai, keeper of the women, who was especially pleased with her. He quickly gave her the beauty preparations to prepare her to go before the king (verse 12). Seven maidens were chosen to attend her, and she was moved into the best place of the house of women. Apparently, there were various degrees of honor among the women of the harem, and from the beginning Esther was given a favored standing.

2:10,11 – Mordecai urged Esther not to reveal that she was a Jew. He showed great interest in her well-being.

To this point Esther had not revealed to anyone in the palace that she was Jewish. Presumably this would have hindered her chances of being selected as queen. So Mordecai had warned her not to speak about her nationality, and she obeyed him (compare verse 20). This shows that Esther and Mordecai were attempting to have her chosen queen; if not, they could have easily eliminated her selection by revealing her nationality.

Mordecai apparently had access at least to the courtyard of the house of women. This appears to have been the consequence of his position, whatever it was. It would not have been because of his relationship to Esther, for had that been revealed it would have identified her as a Jew (we will see that Mordecai was known to be a Jew).

So Mordecai went everyday to pace in front of the court of the women's quarters. There he sought to learn about Esther's well being, though we are not told exactly how they communicated.

2:12-14 – Maidens in turn were given preparations then spent the evening with the king to see whom he might choose.

These verses describe how a queen would be selected from among the young maidens.

Each young woman was given twelve months to prepare before going in to see the king. She would receive six months' treatment with oil of myrrh followed by six months' treatment with perfumes and other preparations. The details are not stated except that this was a procedure every woman went through to beautify her to meet the king. Remember, this was the king of the greatest empire on earth!

After a woman had completed her preparation, she would be appointed an evening to spend with the king. She could have anything she wanted to take with her to attempt to impress the king. No doubt many would choose special clothing, jewels, or other ornaments.

When a virgin's turn came, she would go to the king in the evening, then after she returned in the morning she would go to a second house. The first house was for women being prepared for their first visit with the king. This second house was for women in the harem who had already seen the king at least once. It was under the custody of a different chamberlain named Shaashgaz.

A woman in this second house could go to visit the king again only if he called for her by name. Apparently in the meantime they would simply live there as part of the harem. In this way the king could have more than one visit with a woman, either to get to know her better in his choice of a queen, or just to enjoy her. Doubtless, even after a queen was selected, the king could still choose to spend any given night with any woman in his harem of his choosing.

2:15,16 – When Esther's turn came, she requested only what the custodian advised her for preparations.

Esther's turn to visit the king came in the seventh year of his reign in the tenth month (named Tebeth). This would have been four years after Vashti was deposed (compare 1:3).

When Esther's turn came to go before the king (we are here told her father's name was Abihail), she did not ask for anything special to take with her. She took only the things that Hegai the custodian advised her to take. Yet her beauty and charm were such that she obtained favor of all who saw her even without special aids.

2:17,18 – Esther pleased the king more than the others, so she was chosen as queen.

Esther so impressed Ahasuerus that she obtained grace and favor before him above all the other maidens. He loved her above all the other women and determined to make her queen and set the crown upon her head in place of Vashti.

To celebrate the crowning of the new queen, the king held a great feast for his officials and servants in her honor. He proclaimed a holiday and gave gifts to the people.

Notes about Esther's marriage to Ahasuerus:

1) We may ask whether it was proper for Esther to marry a divorced man. But we must remember this occurred under the Old Testament, in which God tolerated divorce and remarriage as well as plural wives. Consider the cases of David and Solomon, and compare Matthew 19:3-9; 5:31,32; etc. Jesus explained that the Mosaic Law tolerated such conduct because of the hardness of the people's hearts, though it was not what God had originally intended.

Today, however, a marriage like that of Esther to Ahasuerus would be adultery, since Jesus' teaching returned to God's original marriage law of one man for one woman for life (except if one divorces a spouse for fornication). If one divorces for any other cause and remarries, the remarriage is adultery (see also Rom. 7:2,3).

For further information, see our articles about divorce and remarriage at our Bible Instruction web site at **www.gospelway.com/instruct/**.

2) We may also wonder why a Jew was permitted to marry a non-Jew in light of the passages forbidding intermarriage to people of other nations under the law. This had been a great concern in the books of Ezra and Nehemiah. See Nehemiah 9:30; 13:23-27; Ezra 9 & 10; Deuteronomy 7:1-5; Joshua 23:12,13; etc. (and see other references and notes on the passages in Ezra and Nehemiah).

Some may wonder if this case was justified as an exception in that God intended to use Esther to save the Jews. But how would Mordecai and Esther know this at the time of the marriage? Should such "end justifies the means" be accepted?

The proper explanation appears to be that the Old Testament prohibited intermarriage, not with people of all other nations, but only with people of the nations that had dwelt in and around Canaan. Those nations were known to be excessively idolatrous. God cast them out of the land and gave it to Israel because the iniquity of those nations was "full." They surrounded Israel and so would be a continual temptation to them. These reasons did not apply to other nations, and the prohibition is nowhere stated regarding them.

2:19,20 – *The king did not know Esther was a Jewess.*

We are told that the event here recorded took place "when virgins were gathered a second time." Esther was queen at the time (verse 22), so this was after the first time that young maidens were gathered to find a queen and Esther had been chosen. Keil concludes there must have been a later time, after Esther was chosen, when maidens were gathered, not to choose a queen, but simply to increase the king's harem.

At this time Mordecai was sitting at the king's gate. Again it is unclear what his position was that kept him there, whether business or government affairs, we are not told.

Again, verse 20 reminds us that Esther still had not made known her nationality. Mordecai had told her to not do this, and she obeyed him even as she had when he was bringing her up. This fact becomes significant in the subsequent story.

2:21-23 – *Mordecai saved the king's life by revealing a plot against him by two of his eunuchs.*

Somehow, as he was about his business at the gate, Mordecai learned of a plot by two eunuchs, Bigthan and Teresh, who intended to kill the king. They were doorkeepers, so in some sense they were responsible to guard the doors. They became very angry at the king and sought to lay hands on him.

Mordecai learned of the plot and revealed it to Esther. She in turn warned the king, giving Mordecai credit as her source of information (she could do this without revealing her relationship to him).

The accusation was investigated and determined to be true. The men were then hung on a gallows, and the king's life was spared. All this was then recorded in the chronicles, the official record of royal history.

This event also reveals the admirable character of Mordecai. The story may seem to be told here just for the sake of interest, but we will later learn that it plays a major role in the subsequent story.

Esther Chapter 3

The Rise of Haman to Power and His Decree Against the Jews – Chapter 3-5

Haman Decrees the Death of the Jews - Chapter 3

3:1,2 – *Haman was promoted above all other princes, so everyone except Mordecai bowed to him.*

The events recorded here occurred sometime later, after Esther had become queen and after Mordecai had saved the king's life (we are not told how long after). There arose to prominence a man named Haman. He was the son of Hammedatha, an Agagite. Exactly what this tells us about his background is unclear (compare verses 2-4). The king exalted Haman till he was above all the princes of all the provinces. In such a great Empire, this was surely a very exalted position.

As part of Haman's exalted position, the king's servants were required to bow to him and pay homage. This was done at the command of the king.

However, we are told that Mordecai for some reason refused to bow. The reason is not given here but will be discussed more fully in the following verses. This refusal of Mordecai resulted in serious conflict that became the basis of the entire story of the book.

3:3,4 – *The king's servants asked the reasons for Mordecai's stand, and reported to Haman that Mordecai was a Jew.*

Mordecai was then asked, by other of the king's servants who sat in the gate, why he acted in this way, especially since he was disobeying the king's command. He was disregarding, not just Haman, but the king himself. The account does not record his exact answer, but verse 4 shows that his explanation was based on the fact he was a Jew. This

Study Notes on Ezra, Nehemiah, & Esther

plus the fact that Haman determined to slay all Jews (verse 6) shows that Mordecai's reason for refusing to bow was based on his religion and nationality as a Jew. Clearly, a reason of this nature would be required to explain the strength of Mordecai's convictions.

The servants spoke to Mordecai every day questioning him about his conduct, but he refused to listen. Finally, the servants reported to Haman about Mordecai's conduct, to see whether or not Mordecai was going to be able to succeed in his defiance of the law.

The record does not explain why, as a Jew, Mordecai believed he could not bow to Haman. Jews did at times bow to kings – 2 Sam. 14:4; 18:28; 1 Kings 1:16; etc. Two common explanations exist:

(1) Rulers of heathen empires were at times (though not always) honored as gods (compare Acts 12). So bowing to the rulers was viewed as worship or reverence to a deity. If this was the intent in Haman's case, Jews could not participate since it would be idolatry. In this case, however, it is strange that such homage would be required toward Haman, but nothing mentions that such homage was required toward the king himself.

(2) It is possible that "Agagite" means Haman was a descendant of the Amalekites, whose kings were called "Agag" (compare Pharaohs, Caesar, Herod, etc.; see 1 Samuel 15). If so, God had commanded what attitude Jews should have toward Amalekites – Exodus 17:14,15; Deuteronomy 25:17-19.

Lessons from Mordecai's example

The example of Mordecai is worthy of our consideration and imitation. From him we can learn the importance of standing for God's will regardless of the opposition. He refused to sin or violate his conscience despite the great forces that were brought against him.

(1) First, he was disobeying a direct command of the king (compare Acts 5:29).

(2) He had to withstand the continual urging of his companions, who sought to pressure him to participate (verses 3,4).

(3) He was clearly in the minority, perhaps completely alone, in the stand he took. Surely his conduct would be noticed in any crowd, since all the others would be bowing when he would not (the comments of his companions show that others did notice).

(4) He was threatened with death, not just to himself, but to all his people. But even after this decree was officially signed, he still refused to bow (5:9).

Other Bible characters have stood with equal courage in the face of opposition. Daniel refused to eat the king's dainties or to cease praying though it meant being cast into a lion's den. The three Hebrews refused to bow to Nebuchadnezzar's image, though the penalty was the fiery furnace. Joseph refused to commit adultery with Potiphar's wife, though it meant prison. Peter and John continued preaching Jesus thought it meant beating and imprisonment. So Paul and all the apostles and Stephen were persecuted, as was Jesus Himself.

Many of us would have given in to the pressure and excused our participation as being just as "a little matter." But examples such as that of Mordecai should give us courage. We should consider also our own influence on others for good or bad.

Will we stand up and do right when: (1) we are made fun of for teaching others about Jesus? (2) we are called "chicken," "holy Joe," etc. for refusing to practice sin? (3) we are persecuted and even threatened with physical violence? (4) our job is threatened because we refuse to lie, cheat, give to United Way, etc.?

3:5,6 – When Mordecai continued to refuse to bow, Haman determined to destroy all the Jews.

When Haman realized what Mordecai was doing, he became fiercely angry. He wanted to lay hands on Mordecai, but he decided not to, because he had been told that Mordecai was a Jew. Presumably, he understood that Mordecai's religion/nationality was the reason for his refusal to bow. He decided that, rather than just attempting to lay hands on Mordecai, he would attempt to destroy all the Jews in the whole empire.

Note the pride and cruelty of this man:

(1) Note Haman's pride: It was not enough that he was honored with such a high position and such favor with the king. In spite of this, his anger burned over so little a thing as a man who would not bow to him (compare 5:11-13).

Many people cannot handle honor without becoming proud and conceited. They become tyrants who demand cowering submission by their subjects. Likewise, people today are often easily offended when people do not honor and praise them as they think they ought to be. Compare Romans 12:3-5; Philippians 2:2-5; Proverbs 6:16-19; 16:5,18; 13:10; 1 John 2:15-17; Romans 1:30,32; James 4:6; 1 Peter 5:5; 1 Corinthians 13:4,5; 2 Timothy 3:2; Luke 14:7-11; Galatians 6:1; Colossians 3:12,13.

(2) Note Haman's cruelty: It would have been bad enough had he sought to imprison one man to satisfy his own ego. Worse yet would have been an attempt to slay one man. Yet so great was Haman's cruelty, he would have massacred a whole nationality of people for his pride. And these were law-abiding people, hard workers, etc. Mordecai had proved his loyalty to the king (2:21-23). Yet he would have slain them all because Mordecai did not adequately satisfy his vanity.

3:7 – Haman chose by lot a time to accomplish his plot.

These events occurred in the twelfth year of Ahasuerus, which would have been five years after Esther became queen (2:16ff). Haman then proceeded with his plan.

He began by having the lot ("Pur") cast before him to determine what month and day would be most favorable to attempt his plans. "The lot" throughout the Bible is a means of making decisions by some activity that would appear to be an act of chance (throw dice, toss a coin, etc.). However, it was believed that the gods would make the lot turn out such that it would reveal what was true or best. When inspired men did such by God's guidance, the result would be accurate. But here Haman appealed to his sources, which no doubt were false gods or perhaps even astrologers or magicians. Note that such consultation was probably fairly common by rulers in that day.

The result was that the month chosen was the twelfth month. However, as we will see, this was not a day favorable to Haman's purpose at all. This whole book shows that God watches over and cares for His people. We may suffer and be tried, but the final result will be for our good. But false gods cannot defeat God's purpose. Astrology is worthless. All appeals to other sources of supernatural information are inferior. If we want truth, we must go to God and His word.

3:8 – Haman told the king there was a people who did not keep the king's commands nor serve to his profit.

To achieve his goals Haman then went to the king to obtain permission to slaughter the Jews. He stated some partial truths but by no means told the whole truth.

First, he said there was a certain group of people who were scattered throughout the provinces of the empire who, in spite of being scattered, yet persisted in abiding by their own laws that were different than those of other people. This was true in a sense, since they followed God's law. But this was not necessarily bad in any sense.

Haman, however, charged that these people did not keep the king's commands, though he gave no specifics. This may have been true in the sense that they were not bowing to Haman. But in general the Jews were loyal citizens, as Mordecai had shown in sparing the king's life. The Jews' disobedience was hurting no one but Haman! Yet he argued that the people were not profitable to the king, as though this would justify his request. He did not mention his real reason for hating the Jews – the fact that one man would not bow to him, and he was therefore determined to destroy a whole nation! Note the manner in which evil men pursue their goals by half-truths and false insinuations.

3:9 – Haman asked permission to destroy this people and he would pay the king's treasury 10,000 talents of silver.

Having poisoned the king's mind against the people, Haman then boldly requested the destruction of these people. To clinch his request, he offered to give 10,000 talents of silver into the king's treasury if the king would approve the decree (the Waldrons point out that 10,000 talents of silver would equal 375 tons!). This bears all the earmarks of graft and bribery, as is so common in many governments. To pay the king for permission to slaughter thousands of his subjects, however, is the grossest sort of evil! This had been smoothed over, however, by the accusation that the people were rebellious and unprofitable in the kingdom anyway. No information is given regarding where Haman would obtain such a fabulous amount of money. Perhaps he intended to take it from the spoils of the murdered Jews (3:13).

Note that, at this point, Haman had not even identified who these people were that he wanted destroyed. He had not named them as Jews. Nevertheless, the king approved the request. Surely, though, the king learned who it was, at least when the decree was actually issued.

3:10,11 – *The king gave Haman his ring and told him to do as he pleased.*

The king then took his ring, the official seal by which he authorized decrees, and gave it to Haman. The seal was a sign of authority. He thereby authorized Haman to do as he pleased regarding these people, but the king refused the money. He did not want the bribe, but he granted Haman's wish anyway. Apparently he was so favorably inclined toward Haman that he trusted him and simply granted his request without question. He authorized that act at Haman's discretion.

Later the king realized his mistake when he learned the true character of Haman. This should teach us the importance of carefully choosing our close, trusted companions. Haman was an evil companion who corrupted Ahasuerus (1 Corinthians 15:33). We must be very careful what influence people have on us and whose advice we take. Check matters out carefully. Surely in a matter that determined the lives of millions of people, the king should have been more careful and done more investigating. We need to take a lesson from his example.

3:12 – *The decree was written to all the king's provinces.*

Having received authority from the king, Haman acted without delay. On the thirteenth day of the first month the decree began to be written. It was to be executed on the thirteenth day of the twelfth month. This length of time no doubt was helpful to the Jews in giving Esther time to work on the problem.

Haman had a decree written to all the rulers in all the provinces in the language of those provinces. This decree was done by the authority of the king, sealed with his ring. Hence, the people knew they must obey.

3:13-15 – *The decree was published for all Jews to be slain on the thirteenth day of the twelfth month.*

The letters bearing the decree went by courier into all the provinces. The decreed said to destroy, slay, and annihilate all the Jews, young and old, including women and little children. This was to happen on the appointed day, the thirteenth day of the twelfth month. People then were authorized to plunder the possessions of the Jews. The spoil would no doubt serve as a motivation to people to comply with the decree.

Note that the decree, had it been carried out, would have meant virtually the end of the Jewish nation, for it included all provinces, and almost all the world (especially where Jews were) was under this empire. Such would have been a terrible blow to God's people. Would He allow this or would He defend them? Further, consider the consequences to God's plan for man's redemption. If the Jews had been destroyed, how could Jesus be a descendant of Abraham, Jacob, and David as God has promised? No doubt, God could have found a way to accomplish His purpose in any case. But instead He chose to preserve the nation in the manner that we will see.

Note that Haman's evil would not only have affected himself, but he included the king in his evil, and now he was about to include all the people of the empire in his evil. All would have been involved in an act of mass murder. So our sins often affect those around us.

Mass murder, especially of Jews, has often occurred and is always an abomination. Pharaoh decreed destruction of Israelite babies, and so did Herod. Germany murdered millions in Germany. Communists did such a thing in many nations, not just to Jews, but to all who opposed communism. In our own society, abortion is a mass murder of a class of people.

The decree went out by rapid post to inform all the people to get ready for the actual day. The decrees perplexed the people, and rightly so: why murder a whole nationality of people? Why should the people have to be the ones to do it? Who would be the next victims? Meantime, the king and Haman were bosom buddies, drinking together, enjoying themselves, apparently unconcerned about the tremendous impact of their act.

Esther Chapter 4

Mordecai Persuades Esther to Appeal to the King - Chapter 4

4:1 – *Mordecai mourned when he learned of the decree.*

When Mordecai heard of the decree that Haman had influenced the king to make, he felt deep sorrow and mourning. He expressed this by tearing his garment, wearing sackcloth, and crying out with a loud, bitter cry in the midst of the city (presumably publicly).

Mordecai, of all people, should have felt deep sorrow for the decree, since his conduct had occasioned it. Had he alone been threatened for his conduct, that would have been a great enough source of grief. But his conduct had led to a decree of destruction, not just against him or even against his own family, but against the whole Jewish population – all Jews, everywhere on earth. How much greater burden could a man have to bear? Surely it was cause for great sorrow.

Here and in the following story we see another great quality of Mordecai. He felt a deep sense of responsibility for the consequences of his own conduct. Unlike some, he was not indifferent to the suffering or sorrow that could come to others as a consequence of his conduct. It touched his heart, so he determined to do something about it.

Of course, this did not mean Mordecai was convicted that his conduct had been wrong. We will see that he continued to maintain the same conduct. The point is that it grieved him that Haman had reacted so sinfully to Mordecai's stand for truth.

(It may appear at this point that Mordecai did not yet know that his conduct had occasioned the decree, but verse 7 implies he did know.)

4:2,3 – *In every province Jews mourned and fasted.*

He expressed his grief even as far as the gate of the king's palace. He could not, however, enter the gate, because it was against the rules for one who was wearing sackcloth to enter.

Mordecai's grief was shared by Jews in every province. As the decree arrived and was made known, the Jews recognized the danger

Study Notes on Ezra, Nehemiah, & Esther

they faced. They mourned, fasted, wept, and wailed, lying in sackcloth and ashes.

4:4 – *Esther sought to console Mordecai, but he refused.*

To this point Esther had not heard about the decree. She did not yet know that her own husband, influenced by Haman, had decreed the death of all her people! Her servants (maids and eunuchs) were the ones who informed her, but apparently they just told her that the Jews were grieving, perhaps specifically that Mordecai was wearing sackcloth at the gate.

It seems doubtful that these people knew she was a Jew. So far as the record states, she had not yet made this known (2:20). They may have known she had some friendship with Mordecai, or they may have simply informed her of the matter as news (since it had stirred up the whole city – 3:15). Even now it appears that they did not inform her the specifics of the case and its effect on her own people, since Mordecai later explained this to her. But she knew the Jews were grieving, especially Mordecai, and this was enough to cause her distress.

She responded by sending Mordecai better clothing to wear instead of the sackcloth, but he refused it. Apparently she sought simply to comfort and cheer him. But his grief was too great to be so easily set aside. Keil suggests that maybe she offered these garments so that, without the sackcloth, he could then enter the gate and talk to her about what was troubling him. When he refused, however, she found a different way to communicate with him.

4:5-7 – *Mordecai communicated with Esther about the decree through Esther's eunuch.*

When Mordecai refused to be comforted or to come to her, Esther then sent an apparently trusted servant named Hathach to talk to Mordecai. She wanted him to learn the reason for Mordecai's distress.

Hathach accordingly met Mordecai outside the gate in the square of the city. Apparently this was a place of public access, and there Mordecai could go, even in his sackcloth.

Mordecai then explained to Hathach (so he could tell Esther) about the decree and what it would mean. Mordecai, however, knew more than just the decree. By some means he had learned who was responsible and even how much money Haman had offered to pay into the king's treasuries to bring about the Jews' destruction.

I do not know that this means the king had decided to accept the money from Haman (compare 3:9,11). But it would show Esther how devious Haman was and how deeply determined he was to accomplish his purpose.

4:8 – Mordecai sent Esther a copy of the decree and urged her to plead with the king on behalf of her people.

To help Esther see for herself what the problem was, Mordecai even sent her a copy of the decree itself. Note here the value of documenting our statements, especially when they involve an accusation against others. People need to know that our accusations are really true, and there is special power in personal eyewitness of the evidence.

Mordecai then gave instruction to Esther to go herself to talk to the king and appeal to him on behalf of her people. Note that Mordecai did more than just grieve over the problem. He had a plan for dealing with it. He knew Esther was in a position to influence the king, so he asked her to use her situation as a means to benefit God's people. Likewise, when we face difficult circumstances, we may grieve and must ultimately trust God for deliverance, but we should also consider what we can do about the problem and use our opportunities to resolve it.

Note that, at this point, if not before, Hathach would have learned Esther's nationality. The only possible exception would have been if Mordecai had communicated with Esther by means of a sealed letter (though the language does not seem to imply this). If in fact he did learn her nationality, he must have been a trusted servant indeed to keep this matter from eventually coming to the attention of the people, especially the king.

4:9-12 – Esther explained that, if she went before the king without being called, she would be killed unless he held out his scepter.

As a faithful servant, Hathach delivered Mordecai's message to Esther. Esther then responded with a message sent back to Mordecai.

Esther's first reaction to the instruction was much like that of Moses when God called him to go tell Pharaoh to release the Israelites. All she could do was to look at the difficulties and make excuses. And she had good cause for concern! She pointed out that Persian law forbade anyone to enter the inner court where the king was, unless the king called him to come. Any who entered unbidden would be killed, unless the king held out his golden scepter to him. Then the person would be spared to have an audience with the king. So Esther feared to go unbidden to speak to the king.

Further, she pointed out that she had not been called to an audience with the king in the previous thirty days. This would indicate that she foresaw no opportunity to speak to the king – it was not like she had an appointment with him every day! Furthermore, the fact he had not called might indicate he did not particularly desire to see her. This would make it especially dangerous for her to go.

Such objections would naturally arise in anyone's mind in such a case. No doubt there was legitimate cause for concern. One might also remember Ahasuerus' treatment of Vashti as a sign of how he treated queens who displeased him. If Esther's request likewise angered the king, he could easily decide to eliminate another queen and replace her.

Keil wonders why she did not simply send a message to the king and request an audience. This alternative, however, does not appear to have been considered by anyone in the case. Perhaps such was simply not allowed. Or perhaps she feared she would be required to give her reasons for wanting an audience, and that might require her to reveal too much (especially in light of Haman's power) when she was not personally able to plead her case to the king. In any case, this alternative for some reason was not given serious consideration.

Had any of us been in Esther's place, we would no doubt have also been concerned about these problems. Yet it was also clear that such objections would not relieve her of her duty. When we consider the grave consequences to her people, we should clearly see what her duty was. And as Mordecai eventually pointed out, she was destined to die if the decree was carried out and her nationality became known. So why not risk her life now in the hope of saving as many Jews as she could. Doubtless in her heart she knew what her duty was. But like all of us, she hoped to find a different solution that did not involve such danger. How many times do we make excuses facing circumstances of far less consequence!

This message was then delivered to Mordecai.

4:13 – Mordecai reminded Esther that she too would not escape the decree.

Mordecai's response comprises one of the richest sections of the book. Though God is never mentioned, Mordecai's reply reveals deep faith in the providence of God. In stating his views, he helps us to a much deeper understanding and appreciation of God's providence.

Mordecai first reminded Esther of the personal danger she would face if she refused to aid God's people. She herself was a Jew. She need not think, though she was queen, that she would escape perishing with the other Jews. In fact, he assures her that, if she refused to help, she would perish despite the fact he is convinced God would then find some other means to save the Jews (see verse 14).

We too need to consider such lessons as this. We may fear the problems we may face if we serve God, but we need to have a much greater fear of the consequences we will face if we do not serve God (Luke 12:4,5). Yes, people may oppose use, mock us, reject us, or even persecute and kill us if we do God's will. But we will suffer eternally if we do not serve God. Do not think that we can neglect our opportunities to do God's will and yet escape punishment. And do not think we are exceptions to God's laws because we have special privileges in life: power, money, fame, or military might.

Note that Mordecai did not accept Esther's excuses, but neither did he deny the danger. He simply pointed out that the case was such that she must act despite the danger. In much smaller ways (usually), we face similar situations. The case is not that we face no hardships or that we can ignore the hardships. Rather, the nature of the situation is such that we need to act despite the hardships!

Further, Mordecai did not allow his personal attachment to Esther to sway his judgment about what she needed to do. Surely he too recognized the danger she faced, and he was concerned for her. He had raised her and repeatedly proved his love for her. But he overcame his tendency to seek her protection and insisted that she must act despite the danger.

So at times we face situations where natural attachments and emotions might lead us to seek the safety and protection of loved ones. But we must overcome those tendencies when necessary to urge loved ones to act in ways that God's will requires. As with Mordecai, we must remember that they face a worse danger if they disobey God than they do if they displease men.

Esther had made excuses. Mordecai responded by offering encouragement to do right. That is what we must do for other Christians and loved ones. We must not be easily persuaded to give up our stand for what is right, simply because people resist it. We must persist when the will of God is at stake and the consequences are great. People who make excuses at first may yet be persuaded if we persist.

4:14 – *Mordecai said God would surely spare His people, but Esther would perish if she neglected the opportunity.*

Mordecai states his conviction that Esther would suffer if she did not use her position to benefit God's people. He says she and her father's house would perish. Yet even if she did fail to act, he was confident that God would find some other means to save His people.

How could he know this? He knew the Jews were God's people, and the promises of God to Abraham required that his descendants must continue, not be destroyed. Despite his grief, Mordecai knew somehow God must spare the nation so that the promised blessing on all nations (salvation through Christ) must yet come. Many Jews might suffer; many might even be slain. Yet the nation must live on to fulfill God's plan. This is a firm statement of God's providence working in the world to accomplish His purposes.

He also affirmed that Esther may have come to power as queen for the very purpose of being useful to God's purpose as this very time. Compare this to the story of Joseph, who came to political power at the time needed to save the Israelites. Here again was strong evidence of Mordecai's faith in God's providence.

Note lessons we learn here about God's providence.

1) God's power still works in the world, even today, to accomplish His purposes. All that He has promised must come to pass. He is able to make it come to pass. There are things He may determine to do that we do not know what His determination is. But when He has revealed His will, we can be sure that He has the means to bring it to pass (as Mordecai knew God would spare Israel based on His stated promise). So sometimes we can know what He will do, because He has said so. Other times we may not know, because He has not spoken regarding the matter. But we can be sure that He has a plan to carry out His will, and He has the power to work in the Universe to accomplish His will. And we can be sure that, whatever that plan entails, it will be good in the end for those who are faithful to Him.

2) Mordecai also knew that God may use human agents to accomplish His providence, but He does not necessarily depend on any particular human agent. In this way, He does not violate the free will power to choose of any individual. He could use Esther, but she still had the power to choose whether to respond to His will or not. If she chose not to do so, He would use some other agency. God has many resources and many ways to accomplish His will. He is not limited by man's choices, but the choices any individual makes will determine whether God will bless or punish that individual.

3) God is able to work in providence without miraculous means. There is no miracle (an event impossible by natural law) anywhere in the book of Esther, yet it is evident that God is working. So today, the age of miracles has passed. When we teach that, some people argue that the conclusion is that God does not work in the world at all any more. Such statements show ignorance and lack of faith in God's providence. He proves in stories like this that He is perfectly capable of bringing about His will on earth even without miracles. Since miracles have ceased, He is still able by providence through natural law to accomplish His will.

For further information, see our article about miracles and direct revelation at our Bible Instruction web site at www.gospelway.com/instruct/.

4) God may work long in advance of an event in order to have the arrangements made to accomplish His will when the time comes. Mordecai said that Esther may have come to this place of authority for this very purpose. God has the power to know ahead of time what will happen, so He can work as needed to prepare for the situation when it arrives. Then when the time comes, everyone and everything is in place to accomplish His plan.

5) Furthermore, we humans often cannot tell, even when we see events unfold, what God's intentions are; and sometimes we may not even be sure that He is the One who is causing some event. Mordecai

said, "Who knows whether …" He had faith God would accomplish His purpose, but he could not know ahead of time who or what means God would use.

So today people are mistaken when they attempt to read "signs" to reveal God's will for them by interpreting events around them. They are likewise mistaken to claim, based on what they see or experience in life, that "God led me to do such and such," or "I just knew the Holy Spirit was leading me to …" God's will is revealed in Scripture. Other than that, we cannot know what His will and plans are, nor do we know for sure how He is working in any given situation. Nevertheless, though we may not know how, like Mordecai, we can be sure that God is working to achieve His goals.

6) Even though Esther could not be sure God intended to use her, yet Mordecai insisted that she should do what she could do in the circumstance. She should seek to further His cause and aid His people. She had special advantages, so she should use them.

Likewise, we too must use our blessings and advantages to do God's will, even though we may not know how God intends to work out His will here. As parents, we have a unique opportunity to teach our children. As employees, we may influence other workers. If we have wealth, we may support gospel preachers and help the needy. If we are able speakers, we may preach the gospel. If we have singing ability, we may be song leaders. Whatever advantages we have, we should seek to use them for the Lord.

It likewise seems to me that we should use what advantages we have in our nation to help bring about God's will for His people. And we do not have to know for sure what the outcome will be of any situation to do this. Esther used her position as Queen. Paul later used his advantages as a Roman citizen. American Christians should likewise use the advantage we have to vote for candidates that we believe will further decency and good morals. The fact other people do not have these advantages does not excuse us from using them when we do have them, just as the fact other people are not queens did not excuse Esther from using her position as queen. And we do not have to know for sure what God's plans are before we act. Esther did not know God would use her to save His people, but Mordecai still taught that she would be punished if she did not try to use what advantage she had to accomplish God's will.

4:15-17 – Esther urged the people to fast, then she would go before the king. And if she perished, she would perish.

Esther was willing to suffer in order to do what was right.

Having considered Mordecai's appeal and reasoning, Esther sent him her response. She determined that she would go before the king as Mordecai had instructed.

She said, "If I perish, I perish!" We all ought to admire and imitate such courage. We should be willing to serve God according to His will regardless of what price we may have to pay. No matter what the problems, difficulties, or dangers must be, we must proceed. If we perish, we perish. But God will still be pleased and will reward us eternally. Esther's courage should inspire us.

Note she said that such an act would be against the law. Actually, it would be against the law only if the king did not choose to recognize her. But even so, in that case, she would be obeying God rather than men, so it would still be right for her to so act (Acts 5:29). We too should have the courage to violate human law when necessary to obey God.

She first sought God's blessings by fasting.

Before making her request of the king, she determined that she and her servants would fast. And she requested that all the Jews in Shushan join her in this fast. God is not mentioned, but that is the purpose of fasting (see the examples in Ezra and Nehemiah). She seeks to make request of God before she makes request of the king.

This too should be our attitude. Esther was about to work for God, and we have many works we do for Him that we also want Him to bless. Let us appreciate the value of prayer, so we ask His blessings on our work for Him. Sometimes our work too involves some dangers. Let us cast our burdens on Him in prayer. Fasting too can serve a useful purpose in our lives.

Having learned of Esther's decision, Mordecai joined her and did as she requested (i.e., he urged the people to fast on her behalf).

So the scene was set for Esther to go before the king to make request to save her people from destruction.

Esther Chapter 5

Esther's First Banquet for Haman and the King - Chapter 5

5:1 – *Esther put on her royal robes and went before the king.*

On the third day (of the time the Jews fasted – 4:16) Esther made her appearance before the king. She put on her royal apparel and stood in the inner court across from the place where the king sat on his throne. We should appreciate the courage this took, as described in 4:8-17.

Her request would be difficult to make for several reasons: (1) She sought to defeat a decree made by the authority of the king. (2) She knew she had a powerful adversary in Haman, who determinedly hated Mordecai and the Jews. (3) She would have to reveal for the first time that she herself was a Jew. How would the king react to this? (4) Finally, she must go unannounced before the king, an act which of itself would automatically cost her life if the king showed her no favor.

Yet she had resolved to do what was right and needed (4:13-16). She had diligently requested God's blessings on her efforts (4:16). So she then acted courageously on her resolve. So we must do when facing opposition or great responsibility. Let us too proceed when we must preach to influential people, rebuke a brother for sin, stand for our convictions against angry family and friends, etc.

5:2,3 – *The king spared Esther and offered her half of his kingdom.*

When the king saw Esther standing in the court, she found favor in his sight. So he extended the golden scepter to grant her permission to approach him, thereby sparing her life. She came forward and touched the top of the scepter (apparently the proper means of response for one who had been permitted to approach the king).

The first hurdle she so greatly feared had been crossed (4:11). Surely we must see God's providence at work. Note that no miracles had occurred, but her plea had thus far been answered.

Then the king asked Esther what her request was. He promised to give her whatever she asked for, even if she asked for half of his kingdom! What a reception! Surely this was more than Esther dared even hope for, though she still had not reached her ultimate goal.

It is interesting to observe that many of the bad things we fear never really happen. But this is especially true when, like Esther, we put our faith in God. Instead of death, as she feared, she had been offered half of the greatest empire in the world.

5:4 – Esther invited the king and Haman to the first banquet.

Esther did not immediately make known her real request. She simply began by requesting Haman and the king to come to a banquet she had prepared that day.

Here we see great wisdom and patience on Esther's part. It may have been a temptation, after so favorable a reception, to proceed with her ultimate request. But instead, she courted the king's favor and prepared his heart to receive her ultimate request. Her request was great, her purpose momentous, and the need overwhelming. She did not rush to the conclusion but proceeded calmly and wisely.

We should learn from her example, when we attempt such serious matters. Note that she first obtained God's favor by prayer and fasting. Then she courted her husband's favor by a banquet. Then when she had the favor of God and man, she made her request.

Her method pleased the king and led him to look with favor toward her request. It also showed him how seriously she took the matter she was about to request and how much she wanted his favor. And finally, it gave opportunity to seek the most favorable time to speak. Yet consider how much turmoil all this must have cost Esther in the meanwhile!

Note further that Esther realized that "the way to a man's heart is through his stomach." She did not make bold, domineering demands, nor did she nag, nor did she manipulate him, nor did she seek to embarrass him, nor did she whine and complain, as some wives do. She respectfully sought to please him and gain his consent by kind attentions to him. Let godly wives take note!

5:5,6 – The king again offered Esther up to half his kingdom.

Ahasuerus gave order for Haman to be called so they can attend the banquet, as Esther had requested. Both of them were in attendance. (It is interesting how both were available on such short notice. This was providence at work, though it is also possible that Esther checked on the men's schedules before she gave the invitation. If the king could not have attended that day, she would presumably have set another time for them to come.)

At the banquet, the king again asked Esther what her request was. And again he promised to do or give whatever she wanted, even up to half of his kingdom. This shows that he knew that the banquet itself was not the ultimate goal Esther sought. She had some further request to make, and he realized it.

We are told that this is a "banquet of wine," but remember that "wine" in the Bible is not always intoxicating. The same word is used for grape juice, whether fermented or not. See Isaiah 16:10; Jeremiah 48:33; Isaiah 65:8; Genesis 40:9-11; Revelation 19:15.

5:7,8 – Esther invited them to another banquet the next day.

Esther requested simply that the king and Haman come to another banquet the next day. She promised at that time to let the king know her request.

It is difficult to believe that, in making this request for a second banquet, Esther had any purposes other than the same ones she had for requesting the first banquet (see on verse 4 above). Nevertheless, the events that eventually transpired between the two banquets were absolutely essential to the success of her request. This shows how fortunate it was that she requested the second banquet. Once again, God's providence was clearly at work, though even Esther could not have understood it at the time.

5:9 – Haman rejoiced in the queen's banquets, but was furious that Mordecai would not bow to him.

Haman left Esther's first banquet feeling joyful and glad of heart. He had been honored by the queen, who had invited him personally to, not just one banquet, but two! Enjoy it while you can, Haman!

But as he was going home, Haman was confronted with the one great grief of his life. Once again he saw Mordecai at the king's gate. As in the past, Mordecai refused to stand or tremble before Haman – i.e., he refused to give special honor to Haman. This infuriated Haman (compare 3:2).

Note how Mordecai persisted in refusing to bow to Haman. Even after his conduct had motivated Haman to decree the destruction of Mordecai and all the Jews, still he would not do what violated the law of God. Clearly he was deeply upset to see the consequences that could come on the Jews (4:1-4), and he had taken great steps to try to overcome that problem (4:8ff). But the one step he refused to take was to bow to Haman – an act which he was convinced would be sinful. He would stand firm for the law of God regardless of the consequences. We should learn the lesson. How many of us often give in to far less pressure from friends and spiritual enemies!

5:10-12 – Haman bragged to his wife and friends.

Despite his anger at Mordecai, Haman did nothing at the moment. Rather, he went on home and called a gathering of his friends and his wife Zeresh. His purpose, we will see, was to brag about his greatness and bask in the glory of his "fan club." He gave them four proofs of his greatness, all of them material in nature.

(1) He told of his great **riches**. We are not told specifically how rich he was, but apparently his wealth was remarkable enough that he and his friends considered it to be exceptional. He had enough that he had been willing to offer the king ten thousand talents of silver for decreeing the death of the Jews (3:9).

(2) He had a multitude of **children**. Esther 9:10 says he had ten sons. This was enough that he thought it would impress his friends. Note how, in contrast to today, numerous children were then viewed as a great blessing and a sign of eminence (compare the stories of Jacob and Job; Psalms 127,128).

(3) He had great **power and authority**. The king had promoted him and set him above the other officials and servants (compare 3:1,2).

(4) The final proof of Haman's greatness was his **honor**. The proof of this was that he and he alone had been invited to accompany the king to a banquet with the queen. And not only that, but he was invited back to another banquet the next day! This he mistook as a great honor showing that he was above all men in the empire except the king, even in the eyes of the queen.

Here again we see the galling vanity and conceit of this man. He was so stuck on himself and so inflated by his own greatness that he actually called his own brag session! And note that the measure of greatness to him, as with nearly all conceited men, consisted entirely of material pursuits. He considered himself to be great because of apparent success in physical possessions and honors. And note further how he can interpret events such as the invitation to Esther's banquets as having no purpose other than to show his greatness.

Surely we should learn here the lesson of the fleeting and unsatisfying nature of such conceit based on material things. In his very next breath he will acknowledge how unhappy he still is. And we will see further that he is just one day away from complete destruction. Pride goes before a fall. And let him who thinks he stands take heed lest he fall!

5:13 – *Yet Mordecai took away all Haman's joy.*

Having listed all his great honors, Haman then stated his great frustration at Mordecai. All these great honors and blessings, he says, avail nothing to him so long as Mordecai sits at the king's gate – i.e., as long as he continues to just sit there, refusing to rise and do obeisance as others did.

Note how this shows even more the colossal enormity of Haman's ego. Having all these great honors, he was yet not satisfied. It all meant nothing to him, because one little Jew refused to bow to him! It was not enough to have wealth, family, and honor from the whole empire. All these people who did honor him meant nothing to him so long as there was just one man who refused to honor him! The idea seems to be that a man so supremely great as Haman thought he was, should not have to put up with such a sleight and disrespect from anyone, let alone such a dog as Mordecai!

This is typical of vain, greedy human nature. Instead of counting our many blessings, we tend to complain about the insignificant problems we have. Instead of appreciating what we have received, we worry about some minor imperfection in our circumstances.

And note how this demonstrates the failure of material prosperity to satisfy. One would think that someone so richly blessed as Haman would be satisfied. No matter how much we have, those whose joy and happiness in life is found in emphasizing material things think that they would be happy if only they could have just a little bit more. The fact is that material things do not ever really satisfy no matter how much we have. People who seek success in material circumstances will always want more. As long as they see any flaw, minor irritation, or unfulfilled desire, they will not be satisfied!

5:14 – So Haman planned to hang Mordecai on a gallows.

But Haman's "fan club" had a solution for his dilemma! Perhaps he hoped they would come up with a suggestion when he called the meeting. His wife and friends suggested that the simple solution would be to eliminate Mordecai. If he was such a source of irritation to such a great man as Haman, he should just get rid of him! They suggested he build a gallows and then get the king's permission to hang Mordecai on it. Then he could be truly happy and enjoy the banquet with the queen! All this sounded good to Haman, so he had the gallows built fifty cubits (seventy-five feet – seven stories) high!

See again the conceit of Haman and of his friends on his behalf. They all just assume that a man of Haman's great stature has the right to just wipe out anybody who in any way crosses him, just like swatting a fly! And further, they assume that surely a great man like Haman could sway the king to accomplish a little thing like this at Haman's bidding! Then, having satisfied his callous pride by shedding the blood of a righteous man, he could go calmly on and eat a pleasant feast with joy instead of remorse or guilt! See how ego drives a man to such incredible disregard for others. He himself is so important that others are as nothing. He has every right to wipe them out if they so much as cause him a little inconvenience! They are nothing. He is everything!

Note also the danger of bad advice and of having close companionships with people who encourage us in sin and have no scruples against evil. One can be swayed by associates. Haman had influenced Ahasuerus to allow a decree that would wipe out an entire nationality of people. Haman in turn was influenced by his friends to determine to casually slay an innocent man. Note especially the influence of his wife. She could, had she chosen, have been a great blessing to him and given wise counsel. Instead, she became a curse to him by joining in giving evil advice.

Here we see Haman at the pinnacle of his glory and power. Here he was so confident that he had everything under control. All the cards were in his hand. But, "what a difference a day makes." As we enter the next chapter we will see that, unknown to Haman, the circumstances that he interpreted as being proof that he was at the peak of success, actually were the circumstances that would bring him down to total destruction.

Esther Chapter 6

Haman's Defeat & the Jews' Victory – Chapter 6-10

Note that we stand at a dramatic turning point in the story. Up to this point Haman had been rising in power and honor. He had the upper hand and felt assured of success in his efforts to destroy Mordecai and the Jews (5:9-14). We will see how, beginning with this very night, God's providence began to turn all against him. His defeat was so complete that, in one single day he not only failed to achieve his desire to slay Mordecai, but rather he himself fell completely from the king's favor and was slain. Note also how all the story is building to a climax in a single day, as two opposing forces were quite independently seeking the king's favor to achieve totally opposite goals: Haman to slay Mordecai and Esther to deliver Mordecai and all the Jews.

Mordecai Honored for His Loyalty to the King - Chapter 6

6:1,2 – That night the king was reminded that Mordecai had saved him from the plot of those who sought to kill him.

On the very night between the two banquets, on the eve of Esther's request to save the Jews and the eve of Haman's request to kill Mordecai, an event occurred that brought Mordecai (and the Jews) to the king's favor.

The king was unable to sleep that night, so he called for the chronicles of his rulership to be brought and read to him. As the chronicles were read, one event mentioned was the fact that Mordecai had saved the king's life by informing him of the conspiracy of Bigthana and Teresh (2:21ff).

No reason is given why the king could not sleep, but surely God's providence was behind it. See how God uses such small things to bring about great purposes. Again, no miracle was worked, no great

Study Notes on Ezra, Nehemiah, & Esther

impressive ritual, yet God's providence worked one of the greatest deliveries of history (compare 4:14). And one thing God used was the sleeplessness of the king. If God can use such small things for great good, surely He can use you and me!

The importance of the fact this information came to the king's attention at this particular time cannot be over-emphasized. By this means God brought Mordecai to the king's favor at the very time that he needed the king's favor.

Note that Haman had argued for the destruction of the Jews on the grounds they were unprofitable to the king (3:8). Yet here was conclusive proof to the king that one Jew was incredibly profitable to him and had in fact saved his life. Another Jew of great value to him was his queen, but he had yet to learn of her nationality. This information could not have come before the king at a more opportune time, for unknown to the king, both Haman and Esther were about to make great requests of the king both regarding this very Mordecai and his people.

6:3 – The king learned that no reward had been given Mordecai for his good deed.

Having been reminded of Mordecai's loyal service to him, the king wondered what had been done to reward this service. His attendants informed him that no reward had been given. So the king proceeded to search for a suitable reward.

Several lessons should be learned here. First, it was only right for the king to reward Mordecai. People in authority ought to reward those who serve faithfully, not just punish disobedience. Second, we see Mordecai's attitude toward the reward. He seemingly had no bitterness toward the king for having not rewarded him. When he was rewarded, there is no evidence that he became proud or conceited (like Haman) – compare verse 12. He apparently had done service to the king because it was right to do, not because he sought honor from men. Unlike Haman, who later suggested great honors when he thought he would receive them (verses 6ff), Mordecai had apparently made no request whatever for reward. And when none came, he made no complaint to the king.

Finally note, however, that ultimately he received the greatest reward he could hope for. When that reward came, it came at a time that made it far more valuable to Mordecai than any reward that could have been given at the time he did the good deed. Consider the application to our reward. Some want immediate benefits from their conduct, so they emphasize material pursuits. Christians may not receive their rewards immediately, so it may seem (as with Mordecai) that the righteous receive evil, not good, for their reward. But the reward will surely come, and when it does it will be greater than any reward that could be given during this life.

6:4,5 – Haman arrived to ask permission to hang Mordecai.

The king was still trying to think of a good way to reward Mordecai, so he asked who was standing in the court. That is, he wondered who might be present that he could discuss the matter with and get some ideas. Apparently by that time it was day and Haman had come to the palace to make his request for permission from the king to kill Mordecai. So the king's servants told him that Haman was there, so the king ordered to have him brought in.

The irony here is amazing. The king wanted to ask Haman's advice about how to honor Mordecai, yet at that very moment the reason Haman was there was to ask permission to hang Mordecai! From this point on the irony grows.

6:6 – *The king asked Haman for advice about how to honor the man he wanted to reward.*

When Haman had entered, the king placed before Haman the question of what he should do to honor the man whom he sought to honor. The king did not name whom he spoke of, but Haman in his mammoth conceit thought surely the king must be speaking of Haman himself. "Whom would the king delight to honor more than me?" So he thought up the very greatest honor that he himself would like to receive.

Again we see the incredible vanity of this man Haman. First, he did not even ask who was being discussed but simply assumed without evidence that it had to be himself who would be honored. In his conceit, he could not imagine that anyone else deserved to be honored! It would have been bad enough for him to think that no one would be honored above him, but the king had never even said whom he intended to honor. He simply said that he wanted to honor someone. Haman apparently assumed that, beside himself, no one deserved honor!

Second, thinking he would be honored, he presumptuously sought the greatest honor he could think of, instead of humbly seeking little or no honor. He was a glutton for honor. He had just spent an evening boasting to his family and friends about his own greatness (5:10-14). But was he satisfied with the great honors he had? No! Honor is temporary and, like wealth, one must always seek ever more and more hoping to achieve satisfaction by it.

Now note the irony. Haman sought death for Mordecai and honor for himself. Yet on this very day he would see Mordecai receive the very honor that he sought and invented for himself. And likewise, he himself would receive the very death that he had planned for Mordecai. And all this was by God's providence and answer to prayer.

6:7-9 – Haman suggested parading the man on the king's horse and in the king's garments.

According to his presumptuous vanity, Haman proceeded to suggest great honors to be given, all the while thinking that he himself would receive those honors. So he suggested that the man be clothed in royal garments that the king himself sometimes wore and that he be placed upon a horse that the king himself sometimes rode, the horse having a royal crest placed on its head. Then one of the king's highest nobles should be assigned to lead the horse with its rider throughout the city square proclaiming that this was the way the king honored the man who had pleased him. Such would be comparable to our "ticker-tape parades," though in a way it would be an even greater honor, since it was given at the command of the greatest king on earth. The man in effect would be honored as "king for a day"!

6:10,11 – The king commanded Haman to give this honor to Mordecai and even to lead the horse.

When Haman had given this elaborate description, the king was so pleased by it that he commanded that all that Haman had spoken should be done immediately in every detail with no exceptions. But, instead of this being done to Haman as he expected, it was to be for the honor of Mordecai the Jew! Worse yet (from Haman's viewpoint), Haman was the one to be assigned to give the honor. He had to lead the horse! And that is exactly what Haman did.

Imagine the shame and horror Haman felt when he heard this verdict. Not only would this great honor not be given to him as he had planned, but instead it would be given to the one whom Haman considered to be his greatest enemy. And Haman himself would have to give it. And he had himself invented the whole thing!

The irony abounds. He had come to the king's presence to ask permission to *kill* Mordecai. Instead, he ended up honoring him. He hated Mordecai, because Mordecai refused to honor Haman as Haman thought he deserved. Now, instead of eliminating his rival, Haman must be the one to give him honor! (Compare 5:9,13.)

Note that this decree not only honored Mordecai for his righteous conduct, but (unknown to the king) it simultaneously punished Haman for his vanity. And in reality Haman was punishing himself. This is how sin often acts.

Had Haman not been so conceited in the first place, he would not have been bothered by Mordecai's conduct, Mordecai would not have been his enemy, and he would not have been bothered by having to honor Mordecai. Haman had never really been harmed at all. Yet he was mortally grieved, because his vanity and pride had been wounded. His pride itself was punishing him! It was, in effect, a self-inflicted wound. So sin often does to people, even in this life. Yet neither Mordecai's reward nor Haman's punishment were yet complete.

6:12 – *Haman returned home mourning.*

Having been so honored, Mordecai returned to his previous pursuits at the king's gate. Nothing is said about any great pride on his part as a result of the honor he had received. This contrasted to Haman who let honor so go to his head (5:9-14) that when he felt slighted he was really upset (5:13).

After honoring Mordecai, Haman went home in mourning having covered his head. Why? Who had wronged him? No one! Only his pride had been wounded. When he was honored, he gloated. When others were honored, he pouted and threw a tantrum. In contrast, Mordecai showed no signs of gloating over Haman or bragging to his friends, etc. Instead, he simply went back to doing what he had before.

6:13 – *When Haman told these events to his wife and friends, they predicted Haman's downfall.*

Having returned home, Haman once again calls his wife and friends together and tells them the latest events, as he had the day before (5:9-14). But his story the day before had been all joy and glory (except for Mordecai's refusal to bow to him). Whereas, on this day he sulked and sought solace for his shame.

Amazingly, his wife and friends, who had so praised him the day before, now predicted his downfall! They said that, if Mordecai was of Jewish descent and had begun to prevail, then there was no way Haman could prevail against him but Haman would surely fall before him!

Note the fickleness of friends, especially when they follow a man for the sake of his fame, wealth, and glory. They are fair-weather friends who, as quickly as they flocked to a man in his time of glory, will desert him when he falls.

Yet is not clear how they could be so sure Mordecai would prevail over Haman. They said Mordecai would prevail because he was a Jew. But they had already known Mordecai was a Jew, since that was the reason Haman sought to kill him (5:13,14). So why conclude now that Mordecai would prevail? Perhaps they saw the significance of the turn of events.

Haman had intended to kill Mordecai. But not only had he failed in that purpose, he had actually ended up honoring Mordecai. Perhaps the friends recognized this as an omen of things to come. Perhaps they also remembered the history of past victories of Israelites over their enemies. They were like the "fans" that cheer on an athletic team when victory seems assured, but then turn in disgust when it begins to lose.

6:14 – *Haman was then called to Esther's second banquet.*

Now as the irony multiplies, even as his friends were making their predictions of Haman's downfall, the call came from the king's eunuchs for Haman to attend Esther's second banquet. He obviously was feeling bad – not nearly as wonderful as he had felt the previous day when he received the invitation to this banquet. But still he was totally unaware of what lay ahead for him at the banquet. The worst was yet to come.

Esther Chapter 7

Esther's Request & Haman's Downfall - Chapter 7

The story is building to the climax. The "stage" is now set for Esther's request. She has done all she can to prepare the king to be receptive. The king himself, by God's providence, has a favorable attitude toward Mordecai brought to his mind just this very morning. And Haman has been humbled by having to be the one to honor Mordecai. With this background, the story approaches the second banquet.

7:1,2 – At Esther's second banquet the king again offered to give her up to half his kingdom.

Haman and the king then came to Esther's second banquet, as she had requested. At this point, neither the king nor Haman was aware of the nature of Esther's request.

However, the king again asked Esther what her request was. And he again offered to give her or do for her whatever she wanted, up to half of his kingdom. He had made this offer twice before (5:3,4,6). Now the time had come for Esther to speak.

7:3,4 – Esther requested for her and her people to be spared rather than annihilated.

Esther began her request by speaking respectfully: "If I have found favor in your sight, O king, and if it pleases the king..." It is always proper to show respect to those in proper authority when we make request of them. Mordecai's refusal to bow and show **undue** reverence to Haman would not deny or contradict our responsibility to give civil rulers the honor that is properly due them – Romans 13:1-7.

Esther then requested that her life and that of her people (race or nationality) might be spared, because they had been sold to be killed, destroyed, and annihilated. She requested that her life and her people's life be given in response to her petition. "Sold" seems to refer to Haman's offer to pay the king to allow the Jews' death. She said she would have remained silent if it had been simply a matter that they

Study Notes on Ezra, Nehemiah, & Esther

would become enslaved; but when they were condemned to death, she felt she had to speak.

But in any case, she argued, no amount of price paid could really compensate the loss the king would sustain. This appears to refer to Haman's contention that the people were of no profit to the king (3:8), but if they were killed, he would pay the king (3:9). So Esther claims the people were of great profit to the king such that no amount of compensation could really make up for it.

Notice the courage that Esther had in speaking, because she knew her cause was just and God was with her. She had made preparation wisely and carefully to gain the king's favor. But the time had come to speak. No amount of preparation could avoid the fact that sooner or later she had to speak up.

Likewise, there are times when we need to pray for God's help and make preparations to do God's will. But no amount of prayer or preparation eliminates the need for us to act. Prayer does not remove our responsibility to do what we can in God's work. The time comes when we must ***act***. Let us truly trust in God's power and protection, but let us also realize that often He uses ***our effort*** to accomplish His work, so we must do what is best to bring about the needed result.

7:5 – *The king asked who would dare to do such a thing.*

The king's response was to ask who would be so presumptuous in his heart as to dare to seek to slay all the queen's people. He was clearly angry, and rightly so, that anyone would seek to do such a thing. But remember that he did not know at this point that Esther was a Jew, so he did not realize Haman's involvement (perhaps he did not even know that it was the Jews that Haman had been discussing when he had made his request of the king). Still further, he surely did not yet realize that he himself had been an accessory to the act, since he had given his approval to it. Like David, who could see an act as being evil when it related to someone else's conduct, he did not see his own act as wrong despite his guilt.

7:6 – *Esther identified Haman as the enemy.*

Having been asked directly who had sought to slay her people, Esther then boldly and plainly identified the guilty man: "The adversary and enemy is this wicked Haman!"

Notice that Esther was not unwilling to name the specific individual and state plainly that he was evil. Some people today, even in the church, say such should not be done. They tell us not to name specific religious groups or individuals and say they are guilty of sin. But Esther did so, as did Jesus and His apostles. So we must do when it needs to be done for the cause of truth.

Notice also that Esther accused her adversary to his face. Haman was at this banquet and heard her accusation, because she herself had invited him. This gave him an opportunity to defend himself and present his side of the story, if he so chose. She could have chosen to invite only the king, so she could manipulate and politic against Haman behind his back. But she chose rather to confront the issue before the king in the presence of the one she accused. She treated Haman fairly despite the gross and criminal mistreatment he had himself committed against Esther's cousin Mordecai and the whole Jewish people. So we ought to fairly treat even those who oppose us. We should plainly speak against their error, but we should do so fairly.

Having heard the queen's accusation, Haman was terrified. Note how quickly his boasting vanity had changed to cowardice. The man had not considered, when he determined to make the decree, whom all it might affect. He had sought to destroy Mordecai and all his people. Since then he had learned the great favor that Mordecai had before the king, and here he came face to face with the fact that his decree would also lead to the destruction of the queen herself! And the king had just, in Haman's hearing, repeatedly promised to give the queen anything she wants!

Haughty men tend to over-estimate their power. This is one reason why pride goes before a fall. Haman had been so proud of the fact that Esther had invited him to these banquets, but here he realized too late that his decree had far more wide-reaching consequences than he had anticipated. What had seemed to him, in his vanity, to be an easy thing to accomplish, he now realized may be well beyond his ability to carry out. In fact, it was becoming clear that he might be the one to be destroyed. Especially such consequences follow when one is proud against the Lord.

7:7 – Haman pled with Esther to spare his life.

Having heard the evidence against Haman, whom he had previously favored highly, the king in anger arose, left the banquet, and went for a walk in the palace garden. No doubt he felt angry, not only because Haman had issued a decree that, if carried out, would kill the queen, but also doubtless because Haman had betrayed his trust. He had granted Haman high position and great power and had allowed Haman to issue the death decree as he saw fit, but now the king realized how Haman had betrayed his trust and abused his power. He saw now, presumably for the first time, the tragic danger of allowing a trusted counselor to issue a death decree without himself carefully checking out the consequences.

Rather than making a foolish decision, however, as he had done when Haman had asked to issue the decree, the king this time showed wisdom. Rather than acting rashly, he left the room to consider the matter more carefully before making a decision that he might later regret. It is wise for all people, especially those in authority over other people, to carefully weigh important decisions rather than jumping to conclusions.

When the king had left, Haman realized that the king had turned against him and the result could only be harm for Haman. So while the king was gone, Haman appealed to the queen to spare his life.

How interesting and ironic all this is! Just one day earlier all was going well for Haman (so he thought), all had to bow to him and honor him, and his only problem was that one miserable Jew would not bow to him. Now one day later here he was having to prostrate himself before a Jew. One day earlier he had exalted and bragged what a great honor it was to him to attend the queen's banquets. Now one day later he realized that the banquets would lead to his downfall and perhaps even his death. One day earlier he was so confident in his power and position that he thought he could take the lives of all his enemies and decree the death of Mordecai for having crossed him. Now one day later, he must beg a Jew to spare his own life!

And then notice how quickly cruel men can become convinced to believe in the value of mercy! When he was in power and thought no one could stop him, he had no mercy whatever on the Jews. He mercilessly decreed them all to die. He had no mercy whatever on Mordecai but built a gallows to hang him. But now, when he was the one about to fall from favor and perhaps lose his life, suddenly he became a great believer in mercy! What a difference it makes whose foot the shoe is on!

Furthermore, see how quickly some people can be converted to a pro-life view! Haman thought nothing of decreeing the murder of millions of Jews. To order the hanging of Mordecai was but a snap of the fingers to him. But when his own life hung in the balance, suddenly death was a terrible thing!

Likewise, today many people have no scruples against supporting the infanticide of millions of unborn babies. Lawmakers vote for it. Judges uphold it. Society leaders and educators defend it. Organizations operate clinics and become fabulously wealthy practicing it. And citizens by the millions support the practice or at least think nothing of it. But one wonders how quickly they would be convinced to oppose death if, like Haman, they suddenly found their own lives endangered. (No, I am not encouraging violence against any such people; I am simply showing the fallacy of their view.)

7:8 – *The king suspected Haman of violence against Esther.*

Haman even prostrated himself on Esther's couch as he pled for his life. When the king returned from walking in the garden, he saw Haman and thought he was about to do violence to the queen right in the palace, almost before his very eyes. This, of course, was "the icing on the cake," and angered him to the point of reaching a final verdict against Haman.

The word translated "assault" (NKJV) may otherwise imply rape, but surely the king did not suspect Haman of such a thing at this time and circumstance. However, the king might well suspect Haman of seeking to do violence to Esther for having accused him before the king. He may have thought Haman was trying to force Esther to withdraw her accusation or just that he was seeking vengeance on her in anger.

Again, see how quickly one can fall from favor and the severe consequences when it happened. When Haman had been in favor with the king, the king had interpreted everything he did favorably, even allowing him to decree the death of a group of people without suspecting him of wrong. Now the king's anger leads him to interpret even innocent acts as being evil.

When we have a reputation for doing wrong, people put a bad construction on even our innocent acts. When we have told a lie, people suspect us of lying even when we tell the truth. When we have done violence to others, people fear us even when we have no thoughts of harming them. When a man is known to have committed adultery, his wife and others suspect him of attempting further unfaithfulness anytime he is around another woman. This is why a good reputation is so important. When we have betrayed people's trust, they no longer know when to believe us and when to doubt us.

As the king spoke, his servants covered Haman's face. This evidently was symbolic as a sign of humiliation and condemnation, perhaps even a sign that they recognized Haman stood condemned to death. The servants evidently anticipated from the king's manner and words that Haman was in such disfavor as to be unfit to look upon.

7:9,10 – Haman was hung on the gallows he had built for Mordecai.

When a person's evil conduct is exposed, people immediately recall other evil he has done. Every bad act comes to light. In Haman's case, one of the king's eunuchs, named Harbonah, recalled to the king what Haman had intended to do to Mordecai. He recalled that Mordecai had spoken good on the king's behalf (actually had saved his life, as described earlier), but Haman had built a gallows fifty cubits high for the express purpose of hanging this very Mordecai!

Here, even as the king considered what punishment to bring upon Haman, is revealed another conspiracy Haman had committed against another of the king's loyal subjects! Not only had he plotted to annihilate a whole nation of people, which would have included the queen herself, but he had specifically plotted the death of one who had saved the king's life! This was the crowning blow revealing Haman's corruption.

What is more, this situation provided a perfect opportunity for poetic justice against Haman. The king decreed that Haman be hung on the gallows he had built for Mordecai! This is exactly what was done, thereby satisfying the king's anger. So here we have the great and final irony in Haman's life, that he was hung on the very gallows he had built for Mordecai.

Lessons from the Jews' victory over Haman:

Note how, in less that 24 hours, Haman's fate had completely reversed. Surely this shows many lessons to be learned at this point.

1) The power of God's providence – With no miracles, using only natural means including many seemingly insignificant events, using human agents yet without violating any human power to choose, working often in ways no human could have perceived at the time, God accomplished His goal and cared for His people. This perfectly illustrates all elements of providence.

2) The importance of trusting God – Haman apparently had all the advantages and blessings though he had no respect for God's will. Esther and Mordecai trusted God though they had virtually no advantages or reason for hope. Yet those who trusted God prevailed in the end.

3) The justice of God – In the end, evil men are punished and the righteous are exalted. In this case this result occurred in this life, but if it does not come in this life, then it will in eternity.

Esther Chapter 8

The Decree to Spare the Jews Is Issued - Chapter 8

8:1,2 – *The king put Mordecai in Haman's place and Esther over Haman's house.*

Esther given authority over Haman's house

At this point in the story, Haman had fallen from favor and been slain. However, there is more to the story. We will see even further the greatness of the victory of Esther and Mordecai over Haman's treachery.

First, the king set Esther herself in charge over Haman's house. She was given the great wealth that he had bragged so much about. (I'm not sure how much else was involved in being over Haman's house.) Not only did Haman lose his position and honor that had led to such pride, but he also lost all his wealth to one of the very people whom he had sought to destroy!

Mordecai exalted to Haman's position

But honor was given, not just to Esther, but also to Mordecai. He was advanced to high position before the king. This occurred, not only because of the good he had formerly done in sparing the king's life, but also because Esther told the king about Mordecai's relationship to her. This had not been made known till this point, when Esther revealed her nationality.

For all these reasons, the king then exalted Mordecai to the very position that Haman had occupied. The ring, which was the symbol of the king's authority and which had been given to Haman, was here given instead to Mordecai. This showed that he was the most exalted of all the king's ministers.

Further, Esther, who had been set over the house of Haman (verse 1), in turn put Mordecai over that house. All this simply demonstrates that the exaltation, which Haman formerly possessed, now belonged in every detail to the very one whom he considered his chief enemy and whom he had sought to kill. But Haman had been slain in the very manner in which he had intended to slay Mordecai. The reversal is here complete.

There still remained, however, one major problem that had not yet been overcome. We must yet consider how it can be reversed. Haman himself, the issuer of the decree of death to the Jews, had been slain. But the decree itself yet stood. The real root problem had yet to be resolved; only the perpetrator of the problem had fallen.

8:3-6 – Esther requested to reverse Haman's decree.

In tears Esther approached the king again and even fell at his feet, imploring him to counteract the decree that had been made by Haman against the Jews. At first she did as she had done before: she came into the court of the king uninvited, hoping that he would call her forward, rather than allow her to be slain (compare 5:1ff). (It appears that we are here informed first what her purpose was in going before the king, but she actually makes this known to the king in v5.)

As before, the king held out the golden censer to Esther, granting her the right to speak and not die. She then arose and respectfully asked, according to the king's will, if he was truly pleased with her, if he could write letters to revoke the decree of Haman to annihilate the Jews in all the king's provinces.

The lasting effects of sin

Notice how Haman's decree actually outlived him. He himself was no longer able to pursue his vindictiveness against the Jews and had even been slain, yet the effect of his wickedness lived on. So with us, the effect of our sins may continue on affecting our lives or the lives of others even after we have repented or even died.

For example, we may live in sin when our children are small; we may later repent and become faithful, yet they may choose to continue in sin. We may teach false doctrine and later learn the truth and repent, but the people we taught the error may refuse to change. We may drink or smoke for years then later quit, but our body may yet be so diseased that it cannot be healed; or the family that was destroyed by our drinking may never be restored. We may squander our wealth in riotous living, then later repent and be forgiven, yet the wealth is gone, our job may be lost, etc. We may commit adultery then repent, but we must still care of the child we conceived out of wedlock or our spouse may refuse to trust us and determine to divorce us. We may commit murder, but our repentance will not bring the victim back to life. We may commit a crime, but repentance will not free us from prison.

Esther's concern for her people

Esther explained further to the king her motives for her request. She could not stand to see such evil and destruction perpetrated on her people (compare 7:3,4). Surely it was this love and concern that motivated her to act so bravely on their behalf (4:8-16).

Here is another important lesson for us. We have a grave responsibility to save people around us from destruction. Consider how much more serious is the destruction caused by sin than even that of physical death. If Esther needed to speak out to save her people from death, how much more do we need to save those around us from sin? If we have love and concern as Esther did, we must speak. To fail to speak is to demonstrate that we don't really care for their souls. It is interesting how much effort people are willing to expend to save people from physical danger, yet we do little or nothing when the face the far greater danger of eternal destruction for sin!

8:7,8 – The king granted permission for a new decree.

The king then reminded Esther and Mordecai that he had hung Haman and put Esther over his house, because Haman had opposed the Jews. It is unclear whether the king said this to rationalize his own responsibility for the decree against the Jews or whether he was just reassuring them that he was still willing to help further with the problem.

In any case, he then gave them blanket permission to issue whatever decree they wish to make, write it in his name, and seal it with his ring. The one thing they had to remember, however, was that the law of a Persian king could never be reversed once it had been issued in his name and sealed with his ring. This meant, first, that they could not directly revoke the previous decree; it must be allowed to stand, so they must find some other means to solve the problem.

The second application of this was that their decree would also be irrevocable. So they should be sure that it was just, realizing that it too could not be reversed. They should not repeat the error of Haman in issuing an unwise decree. This also meant, however, that once they made a new decree, no one in the kingdom could prevent them from carrying it out.

8:9,10 – Mordecai and Esther issued a new decree and had it sent to all provinces in the realm.

Once again the scribes were called to issue another decree. This occurred on the twenty-third day of the third month. This means it was two months and ten days since the original decree had been issued (3:7,12). This decree was also to be sent to the Jews and to all the rulers in all the provinces, according to their own language, just as had been done with the original decree (3:12). In addition, we are given further information regarding the size of the empire: it included 127 provinces from India to Ethiopia.

The decree was written again in the king's name, sealed with his ring, and sent out by his couriers, who rode swiftly on royal horses. This was also how the first decree had gone out (3:15).

8:11-14 – The decree allowed the Jews to defend themselves and to plunder any who attacked them.

Here we are given the substance of the decree Esther and Mordecai wrote. The decree could not reverse the fact that the Jews' enemies had been given permission to attack them, since the previous decree was irrevocable (verse 8). So the new decree gave the Jews the right to use force to defend and protect themselves against their enemies, and in fact, they could even kill and plunder anyone who attacked them. The previous decree had granted the Jews' enemies the right to kill and plunder the Jews. This decree gave the Jews the right to do the same to anyone who did choose to assault them.

It is unclear to me whether this means that they could only act in strict self-defense, slaying only those who physically attacked them on this day, or whether it also granted them the right to take offensive action and attack any who had wronged them in times past or those who might have originally planned to attack them under the original decree (even if they now were to change their mind). It seems that they did the latter, though I am not sure. Such wars were fought at various times by the nation of Israel under the Old Testament. (Note: The latter course would have been as wrong on their part as Haman's original decree had been, but for the fact that these enemies were known to be evil, opposing God's will and His people.)

The day on which the Jews could do this was the same day that Haman had originally decreed for people to destroy the Jews – the thirteenth day of the twelfth month (compare 3:13). All this, of course, did not technically reverse the original decree, but it had that effect in the end. The original decree had said nothing about whether or not the Jews would be allowed to defend themselves and even to attack those who attacked them. This decree defined that they could strike back against those who attacked them.

We will see, however, that the effect was much greater than that. The effect of the original decree would have been to put all the force of the empire behind those who would attack the Jews. Their enemies would have been openly and officially encouraged by the government of the empire to attack the Jews, and probably the empire's armies and officials would have been encouraged to join in. All who did so would receive the spoils. Now, however, this part would be effectively reversed. It was now clear that the force of the empire was on the Jews' side and against their enemies.

This decree was written and circulated throughout the empire, so the Jews could make ready for the appointed time.

8:15-17 – The Jews rejoiced in the new decree.

Mordecai had been exalted to such high position that he was provided apparel to show his position. His clothing was royal apparel of blue and white colors. He wore a great golden crown and also a garment of purple color made from fine linen (probably a robe or outer garment).

Whereas the original decree had caused great consternation among the people, this one led to great joy and gladness, even in the city of Shushan. The Jews especially rejoiced with gladness and honor. This was easily understandable considering the seriousness of the original decree.

As news of the decree spread to every province and city, the Jews there would rejoice with feasting and gladness. The result was (as mentioned above) that great fear fell on all the people because of the Jews (this would lead them to fear to attack the Jews on the decreed day and would even lead many to fight on the Jews' side).

In fact, many people even became Jews. This is a clear reference to the practice of proselytes to the Jewish religion. People born as descendants of the Jews were automatically in covenant relationship, but here we are clearly shown that other people could also join the religion.

However, it is not easy to be sure of the motives of these people. It could mean that people converted to Judaism in order to enjoy the honor and wealth that the Jews would receive when the decreed day occurred. Such would be a completely unacceptable reason for converting, since it showed no honor to God. On the other hand, it could be that the people saw that the events that had occurred proved that God was with the Jews. They had seen evidence of His power working in the Jewish nation, so they believed in the God the Jews worshiped.

Esther Chapter 9

The Jews Slay Their Enemies - 9:1-18

9:1,2 – *The day arrived for the edict to be carried out.*

The day that Haman had appointed for the Jews to be destroyed was the thirteenth day of the twelfth month of the year (Adar). This was the day appointed in the command that Haman had decreed by the authority of the king (compare 3:13). That decree could not be changed, so on that day the enemies had authority to attack and destroy the Jews. However, at the influence of Esther and Mordecai, a new decree had been issued that on that day the Jews could not only defend themselves but could even slay those who hated them and had wanted to destroy them (8:11,12). So this was the day that the Jews' enemies had hoped to overpower and slay them, but instead the opposite happened and the Jews overpowered and slew their enemies.

In theory, the Jews' enemies could still have prevailed against them, but the reasons why the Jews prevailed are explained as the story enfolds. The Jews gathered together in the cities throughout the provinces of Persia to fight against their enemies. This enabled them to take advantage of the strength of numbers, rather than being attacked individually.

But specifically mentioned is the fact that the fear of the Jews had fallen on all the people. This was probably due to the fate of Haman and the power of Mordecai, as discussed further in the following verses. People had just become convinced that the Jews' enemies would not prevail, so they tended to be afraid to attack them.

9:3-5 – *Government officials helped the Jews, so they defeated their enemies.*

Another reason the Jews prevailed was that government officials assisted them. In fact, all the people involved in the king's service helped the Jews. The reason is stated: they recognized and feared the power and influence of Mordecai.

Had Haman still been in power, the people would have believed that they could attack the Jews without harm coming to them. The government would have been behind their attacks, approving it and perhaps even helping in it. But now that Haman had fallen and Mordecai had come to power, the people feared to oppose Mordecai's power. The government now stood with Mordecai, so government agents helped the Jews instead of their enemies.

The influence of Mordecai

The reason the people feared to oppose Mordecai was, as v4 says, because he was great, increasingly prominent, and his fame had spread throughout the provinces of the empire. This led people to fear to oppose the Jews, so the Jews were able to defeat their enemies with slaughter and destruction as they willed without successful opposition.

9:6-10 – Jews' enemies were defeated in the citadel Shushan.

Those whom the Jews killed included five hundred people just in the citadel of Shushan itself where the king lived. Included among this number were the ten sons of Haman, who are named in these verses. Haman had sought to slay all the Jews, and he had been extremely proud of all his sons (5:11). But in the end not only did he die, but all his sons also were slain.

We are told, however, that the Jews did not touch the plunder. That is, they took no spoils from those they killed. This is repeated in verses 15,16. The decree that had been issued expressly allowed them to plunder their enemies (see 8:11), but they chose not to do so. Perhaps this was done to show that they did not act from a desire for wealth – theirs was not an attack of aggression for their own gain. Their motives were entirely based on self-defense and protection against those who had sought to harm them.

9:11-14 – Another day was granted for the Jews to defeat their enemies and Haman's sons were hung.

The king was informed how many people had been killed in the citadel of Shushan (see verse 6). He then informed Esther of this and of the death of the ten sons of Haman. At that point he did not know how many had been killed elsewhere, but he wondered how many there would be if this many had been killed in the citadel alone.

He then asked Esther what else she would like to have done. Whatever further request she had, he was still willing to grant it.

A decree for another day of slaughter

Esther's response was: first, she sought yet another day for the Jews to fight against their enemies; but this applied just in Shushan the citadel, not throughout the empire as had been the case on the first day. We are not told exactly why she made this request. Perhaps she had heard already of some of the Jews' enemies who had escaped the first day of slaughter. This would seem to make it clear that the Jews did not just kill those who attacked them, but they took aggression against their enemies. If not so, then why seek another day of fighting?

Second, she wanted the ten sons of Haman to be hung on a gallows. Though they were dead, they would be hung even as Haman had been and as he had sought to do to Mordecai. The king agreed to this request too, so the ten sons of Haman were hung on a gallows. Again, we are not told exactly why she made this request. The sons were already dead. The only purpose I can think of was to make a public display to warn potential enemies of the Jews to not seek to harm the Jews as Haman had.

9:15,16 – *The second day of slaughter was followed by rest.*

As had been decreed, the Jews in Shushan (not the rest of the empire) gathered on the fourteenth day of Adar and continued to slaughter their enemies as they had on the thirteenth day of the month. The first day they had killed five hundred enemies, but this time they killed three hundred more. And once again we are told that they took no plunder (see on verse 10).

The Jews in the other provinces had been told to fight their enemies only on the thirteenth day of the month (see verse 17). So, whereas the Jews in Shushan were still fighting their enemies on the fourteenth day, the Jews elsewhere in the empire rested on that day.

But we are told that, altogether, seventy-five thousand enemies of the Jews had been slain around the empire. Nevertheless, again the Jews did not take plunder for themselves.

9:17,18 – *The Jews celebrated days of rest and feasting.*

These verses clarify the timing of the events. Verse 17 shows that the Jews throughout the empire killed the seventy-five thousand enemies on the thirteenth day of the month Adar, as per the decree. Then they rested on the fourteenth day of the month. The Jews in Shushan had fought on both the thirteenth and the fourteenth days, so they rested on the fifteenth day.

So the fourteenth day was a day of feasting and rejoicing for Jews throughout the empire, and the fifteenth day was a day of feasting and rejoicing for the Jews in Shushan. The rest of the chapter then describes how this led to an annual feast for the Jews.

Surely this became a great victory for the Jews. The beginning of the story gave cause for fear that the Jews everywhere might be destroyed. By the end of the story, however, the Jews had won a great victory over their enemies.

Feast of Purim Instituted - 9:19-32

9:19-22 – *The fourteenth and fifteenth days of Adar established as holidays*

The fourteenth day of the month of Adar was celebrated as a holiday for feasting and gladness and for sending presents to one another. But since the Jews in Shushan had celebrated on the fifteenth day of the month, both the fourteenth and fifteenth days came to celebrated as an annual holiday among the Jews.

Mordecai wrote letters to all the Jews throughout the empire of the king that they should establish these two days as an annual celebration. These days had been planned as a day of defeat of the Jews leading to sorrow and mourning, but instead they became days of rest from their enemies. So they were set up as an annual remembrance on which the people would feast, rejoice, and send presents to one another and gifts to the poor.

9:23-25 – *This served as a memorial to the victory Esther achieved over Haman.*

As we have read, Haman had plotted to annihilate all the Jews, but Esther had influenced the king to bring about the fall of Haman and ultimately the death of all his sons. So Haman's plot ended up turning against him. The Jews accepted the decree of Mordecai as a custom in which they remembered this event each year.

Haman had determined this date by the cast of the Pur – i.e., the lot – see on 3:6,7. We will that this led to the name of the annual feast.

9:26-28 – *The feast was designated Purim.*

Because Haman had determined these days by casting the Pur or the lot (verse 24), the Jews then named the annual holiday Purim. They imposed this day on themselves and their descendants as an annual holiday to be celebrated without fail in these two days every year. The days were to be remembered by every family in every city and province in every generation. This was to insure that the memory of these events would be established and would never perish among the Jews.

9:29-32 – *Esther and Mordecai confirmed the feast of Purim.*

Esther then wrote a letter, in addition to the one Mordecai had written, to confirm the celebration of the feast. She had full authority (apparently as queen) to do so. Mordecai then sent letters to the Jews throughout all the provinces of the empire about this.

So the feast of Purim was confirmed and decreed to all Jews and their descendants. This was also then recorded in a book (perhaps the chronicles of the kings of Persia). This feast is still kept today, still called the feast of Purim, in the month of March.